Indiana

**INDIANA
BY ROAD**

Celebrate the States

Indiana

Marlene Targ Brill

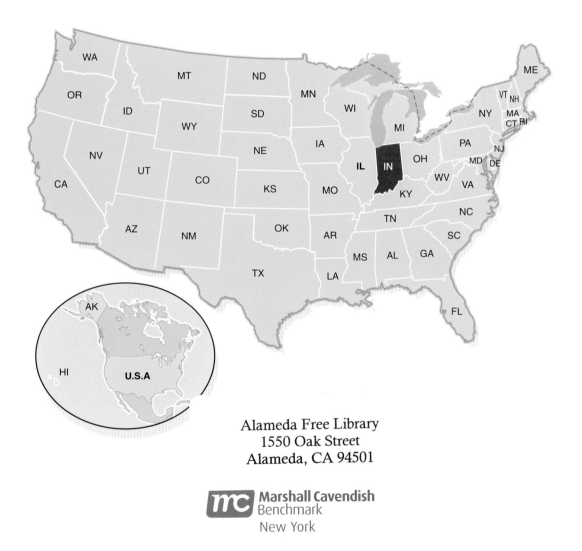

Marshall Cavendish
Benchmark
New York

Marshall Cavendish Benchmark
99 White Plains Road
Tarrytown, New York 10591-9001
www.marshallcavendish.us

Library of Congress Cataloging-in-Publication Data

Brill, Marlene Targ.
Indiana / by Marlene Targ Brill.—2nd ed.
p. cm. — (Celebrate the states)
Summary: "Provides comprehensive information on the geography, history, governmental structure,
economy, cultural diversity, and landmarks of Indiana"—Provided by publisher.
Includes bibliographical references and index.
ISBN: 0-7614-2020-7
1. Indiana—Juvenile literature. I. Title. II. Series.
F526.3.B752006
977.2—dc22   2005015948

Editor: Christine Florie
Editorial Director: Michelle Bisson
Art Director: Anahid Hamparian
Series Designer: Adam Mietlowski

Photo research by Candlepants Incorporated

Cover Photo: David Davis/Index Stock

The photographs in this book are used by permission and through the courtesy of; *SuperStock:* agefoto-
stock, 8; Richard Cummins, 70, 74, 77, 96, 98, back cover. *Index Stock:* Jeff Greenberg, 11, Mark Segal,
108; Ed Lallo, 121; Mark Gibson, 136. *Corbis:* David Muench, 12; Steve Kaufman Bob Rowan, 14;
Layne Kennedy, 15; Patrick Bennett, 16; David Sailors, 19; 21, 32, 49, 87, 105,; Brent Smith, 22; Joel
W. Rogers, 25; Bettmann, 31, 36, 45, 52, 125, 133; Donald C. Johnson, 53; Ralf-Finn Hestoff, 54;
Reuters, 61; Patrick Bennett, 63, 65, 103; Steve Raymer, 66; Ron Sachs, 73; Wally McNamee, 79; Roger
Ressmeyer, 80; Charles E. Rotkin, 82, 86; Steve Liss, 83; Robin Jerstad, 89; Mark E. Gibson, 100; Peter
Smithers, 111(top); Gary W. Carter, 111(low); Ning Chiu, 129; *Photo Researchers Inc.:* David Middleton,
27; Manfred Danegger, 115; Jeff Lapore, 116. *Bridgeman Art Library:* Private Collection/The Stapleton,
28; New York Historical Society, New York, USA, 37. *Indiana Historical Society:* 33,34,41,43; Bass Photo
Co., 42; Madame C.J. Walker Collection, 48. *The Image Works:* Eastcott-Momatiuk, 59; Jeff Greenberg,
69, 138. *Getty Images:* Stefan Zaklin: 75. *Indiana Office of Tourism:* 92.

Printed in China
1 3 5 6 4 2

Contents

People in Indiana have always valued state history . . .

"My father kindled the first fire at Detroit . . . thence extended their line . . . down the Ohio to the mouth of the Wabash."

—Little Turtle, Miami chief, 1795

"We have great history. When kids study Indiana history in fourth grade, they get so excited."

—Tammy Noll, LaGrange teacher

. . . and their natural resources.

"A sense of peace and loveliness never before experienced came over me [upon seeing Brown County]."

—Adolph Shulz, founder of the Nashville art colony

"From sand dunes to streams running in limestone canyons . . . the natural . . . wonders of Indiana come alive."

—William Forgey, Merrillville author and outdoorsman

"The winds of Heaven never spanned
The borders of a better land
Than our own Indiana."

—Sarah T. Bolton, Indianapolis poet

The state claims many creative people.

"I am a woman who came from the cotton fields of the South. . . . I promoted myself into the business of manufacturing hair goods. . . . I have built my own factory on my own ground."

—Madam C. J. Walker, the nation's first black millionaire, Indianapolis

"Indiana is a state where not to be an author is to be distinguished."
—Meredith Nicholson, author, Crawfordsville

Like elsewhere, people may be too stuck in the past . . .

"There's that element of people who believe they're the only ones with truth, and the only ones whose prayers will be heard."
—Philip Goff, Indiana University

"Hoosiers seem a bit backward at times. For example, Indiana refuses to join the rest of the nation and adopt daylight saving time."
—Rebecca Scott, West Lafayette

And they are proud to call Indiana home.

"There's a sense of youth, small-town pride, and a strong feeling of community."
—Raymond Bial, Seymour-born children's author and photographer

"My hometown—not just another pretty place!"
—Garfield the cat, Fairmount-created

Indiana is about as middle America as a state can be. Its people are laid-back and easygoing. They prize the simple things in life—their small towns, sport teams, diverse countryside, and rich history. The different voices of Indiana will surprise you. So will the state's down-home treasures. This is Indiana's story.

Chapter One

Natural Wonders

Millions of years ago massive waters covered the land we call Indiana. As the earth cooled, these seas froze into ice slabs, or glaciers. A series of mile-thick glaciers crawled through central North America. As they crept along, the glaciers flattened mountains, filled valleys, and carved out riverbeds.

When the climate warmed, the glaciers melted and much of the earth dried again. By then glaciers had created a broad flatland and left it topped with layers of crushed rock and clay. Plant and animal remains turned other layers into rich topsoil filled with mineral deposits. For centuries this fertile land attracted settlers to the region now known as Indiana.

HEART OF THE NATION

"Indiana is not Out West or Way Down East or Up North or South in Dixie," wrote Indiana author George Ade. "Rather, it's smack in the middle of America."

And that's what people from Indiana like. Many residents believe their central spot in the nation's Midwest region makes them special.

The dramatic ravines and canyons in Turkey Run State Park were formed by the force of melting glacial waters ten thousand years ago.

People pride themselves on their sense of balance and fair play. Indiana's state motto, "The Crossroads of America," describes Indiana's central location along highways, railroad lines, and water routes. But these words also express the pride residents feel as Middle Americans in the nation's heartland.

Indiana is the smallest of the twelve Midwest states. With about 36,000 square miles, the state ranks thirty-eighth in size. Indiana is considered a northern state, yet its tail dips into the South.

"The glaciers ended here [in southern Indiana] and left the area with caves and sinkholes," said farmer Jane Stuart. "This place is where southern and northern plants meet."

South from Indiana is Kentucky. To the north is Michigan and to the east is Ohio. Illinois is Indiana's neighbor to the west. Inside the stubby, boot-shaped state are three main regions: northern, central, and southern.

Northern Indiana

The north is lake country. About four hundred lakes flow through Indiana's rolling farmland. Lake Michigan—and its forty-five miles of northwestern Indiana shoreline—is the most striking natural feature of the region. Lake winds and waves wash rocks ashore and grind them into sand. Strong currents push more sand from the lake bottom. Together these forces form peaceful sandy beaches and some of the largest sand mountains, or dunes, in North America. The Indiana Dunes National Lakeshore spans eighteen miles along Lake Michigan. The site consists of 14,000 acres of beach, marsh, dunes, and forests, as well as 1,500 species of plants. Two-thirds, or 1,530 acres, of Indiana Dunes State Park is protected by state laws that created and expanded the Dunes Nature Preserve.

The Indiana Dunes National Lakeshore is noted for its quiet beaches, as well as its sand dunes, bogs, marshes, and diverse wildlife.

At 123 feet high, Mount Baldy is the tallest dune in the National Lakeshore. Winds blow the sand mountain south about four feet each year. Currently Mount Baldy is burying an entire oak forest. Hikers claim they hear "singing sand" from its movement when the wind is right.

Inland from the sandy peaks are patches of fertile flatland and wetland. Thick forests of white pine, cedar, oak, and maple cover the northern quarter of the state. These trees are home to such migrating birds as bobwhites, chickadees, warblers, and herring gulls. Foxes, deer, beavers, skunks, mink, and dragonflies play under the trees' sheltering leaves.

Nature lovers especially like Pinhook Bog, also part of the National Lakeshore. Bogs are giant shallow clay bowls that were carved by glaciers and now trap pools of water. At Pinhook, plants grow thick on top of the waterlogged ground. Some of them even eat insects! Children love to jump on the bog to make the mossy ground jiggle.

Thick mats of moss strong enough to support a person, as well as orchids and insect-eating plants, grow on top of a bog in the Dunes National Lakeshore.

BUG-EATING PLANTS

Did you know that some plants eat insects? Three types of bug-eating plants live in Pinhook Bog.

Pitcher plants send water through tubes with hairy linings. When insects come to drink the water or lay eggs in the tubes, they become trapped by the spiny hairs. The bugs rot and are absorbed into the plant.

Sundews (right) have flowers that are smaller than your little fingernail. The flowers form sugary-tasting droplets that attract insects. Because the droplets are sticky, insects get stuck and become tasty treats for the plants.

The bladderwort, a tiny plant, has ten to twenty hollow balls that are slit in the center and hold water. Hairs inside the balls detect motion in the water. When a thirsty insect crawls into one of the balls, the hairs clamp down, trapping the bug inside.

Just east of Pinhook in Lake County is Hoosier Prairie Nature Preserve. More than five hundred acres of natural prairie thrive between urban and agricultural areas. Once the area was covered with sand dunes. Today, wet and dry sections make up marshes, prairies, and white oak grasslands. The region is home to the most varied animal and plant life in the state. Sweet fern, cattails, milkweed, and blue flag appear near Indian grass, rattlesnake master, and wild quinine. Because Hoosier Prairie lies near southern Lake Michigan, more than 120 different kinds of birds migrate there. To protect the plants and animals within, visitors have limited access to most of the preserve.

Central Indiana

Central Indiana is farm country. The region, ranging from flat to gently rolling hills, is called the Till Plains for its rich mixture of gravel and clay soil. Grain and livestock farms reach as far as the eye can see. Every fall huge stretches of farmland are ripe with growing crops.

"I am much pleased with this country," William Henry Harrison, ninth president of the United States, wrote of central Indiana in 1801. "Nothing can exceed its beauty and fertility."

The fertile soil of Central Indiana remains after ice age glaciers brought gravel and clay, creating rich land that now grows corn, soybeans, and other crops.

Only a few rolling hills and winding roads break up the mostly flat farmland. About every fifty miles, however, a clump of trees rises unexpectedly from the open land. Once, hardwood forests spread across 90 percent of the area. When the early settlers arrived, they cleared the land and tilled the soil. Today, only 20 percent of Indiana is forested land.

"Indiana was a wild region with many bears and wild animals in the woods," remembered President Abraham Lincoln. "My father settled in an unbroken forest; and the clearing away of surplus woods was the great task at once."

In southern Indiana the Salem limestone belt runs through most of the region. This stone is preferred when constructing large buildings. The mining of coal and gypsum is also widespread here. This region of wave-shaped hills and lowlands escaped the crushing glaciers and much of the farmer's plow. Today, these scenic mountains have hidden caves that snake through many untouched regions. Wyandotte Caves form the largest underground rooms in the world. The earth in southern Indiana is filled with limestone and contains oil and mineral deposits for mining.

There are more than 2,600 known caves in Southern Indiana. Marengo Cave (above) formed between 700,000 and 1,200,000 years ago.

Of the twenty-three state parks in Indiana, the most striking is the Hoosier National Forest. Its more than 200,000 acres can be found in scattered parcels among the southern portion of the state. Deer, coyotes, badgers, opossums, owls, hawks, foxes, and bears live in the wooded hills. Mineral springs, deep valleys, and ragged ridges attract vacationers and artists to this region. The beauty of forested Brown County inspired the poet James Whitcomb Riley to write "Ain't God good to Indiana?"

Deer make their home in Indiana's Hoosier National Forest.

THE LEGEND OF PIKES PEAK

Indiana's Pikes Peak is named after the famous snowcapped Colorado rise in the Rocky Mountains, even though there isn't a hill within half a mile of the Hoosier area. In *Home Country*, American journalist Ernie Pyle told how Brown County's Pikes Peak got its name. According to legend, a Brown County man got "western fever" in the mid-1880s. He sold his patch of land and all of his furniture and loaded his wagon with several months' worth of supplies. Then he started west with "PIKES PEAK OR BUST" painted on the side of his wagon.

After a couple of weeks the man grew terribly homesick. He returned home but had nothing left except a wagonload of supplies. To raise money, he pitched a tent and sold his supplies from the wagon. Bargain hunters were told to buy them from "that Pikes Peak feller." Brown County residents who came later kept the name.

WATERWAYS TO THE WORLD

A vast network of rivers and lakes contributed to Indiana's motto, "The Crossroads of America." Lake Michigan played a huge role in how northern Indiana developed. Lakeshore harbors opened Indiana to the Atlantic Ocean and beyond through the Great Lakes and into the Saint Lawrence Seaway. Burns Waterway Harbor, on the southern tip of Lake Michigan, became Indiana's only industrial harbor not situated along the Ohio River. Major industries and import-export businesses started there. The lakefront manufacturing district that spread from Illinois to Indiana along the shores of Lake Michigan was named the Calumet region for the Grand Calumet and Little Calumet rivers that run along Indiana borders.

Lake Michigan

Hammond •   • Gary

South Bend •   • Elkhart

Kankakee R.

Fort Wayne •

• Huntington

Tippecanoe R.

Wabash R.

Logansport •

West Lafayette •   Kokomo •   Marion •

• Lafayette

Mississinewa R.

Frankfort •   Muncie •

White R.   Anderson •

Crawfordsville •   Franklin Township (1,257 ft) ▲

Eel R.   Indianapolis   Richmond •

Wabash R.   Brookville Lake

Terre Haute

• Greensburg

Bloomington •   • Columbus

Monroe Lake

Wabash R.   Bedford •   Madison •

White R.   Ohio R.

Vincennes •   Shoals •

Patoka Lake   New Albany

Evansville •   Ohio R.

LAND AND WATER

The most celebrated Indiana waterway, however, is the Wabash River. Countless songs and poems sing its praises. The most famous is the state song, "On the Banks of the Wabash, Far Away," by Paul Dresser. The Wabash forms the boundary between the northern and central regions. It runs southwest across the state to Terre Haute and then southward into the Ohio River, shaping the state's western border with Illinois. The Ohio River separates Indiana from Kentucky to the south. The Wabash and Ohio rivers contributed to Native American and French settlement, and later, to early steamboat travel.

"The river draws him to it like a magnet, and on its banks he will stand for hours, simply watching the water glide past," wrote William Wilson in his novel *The Wabash*.

The Natcher Bridge spans the Ohio River to join Indiana with Kentucky.

Most Indiana rivers drain into the Wabash. The White River runs southwest and meets the Wabash north of Mount Carmel. Other major branches of the Wabash are the Mississinewa, Tippecanoe, and Salamonie. These and several low-level streams fan throughout most of Indiana. Some travel southwesterly all the way to the Mississippi River and then the Gulf of Mexico.

Indiana's waterways, such as the Wabash and Erie Canal and the Whitewater Canal, linked rivers in order to improve shipping and travel. Small towns sprang up along these canal routes before train travel. At first, horse-drawn canal boats and flatboats carried goods and people downriver. Later, steamboats that ran with or against the current made river travel a booming success. Today visitors can view the Whitewater Canal State Historic Site in Franklin County and ride a horse-drawn canal boat.

SEASONS THAT CHANGE

Indiana residents have an old saying: "If you don't like the weather in Indiana, wait five minutes for it to change."

Four distinct seasons determine how much time Indiana residents, or Hoosiers, spend outdoors and what farmers plant. Indiana's hot, muggy summers are well suited for growing tobacco and fruit, and its cold, snowy winters are ideal for snowmobiling. In between, the seasonal colors of autumn and spring lure hikers, bikers, and nature lovers outdoors.

In general, Indiana weather can be humid, rainy, cloudy, or windy at any time of the year. Within each season, climate can vary greatly between the northern and southern parts of the state. One December traveler bundled herself in an overcoat and boots to weather Merrillville's icy streets and twenty-degree temperature. The next day she headed south and roasted under New Harmony's sunny, sixty-degree sky.

When snow arrives, Hoosiers like to ski, snowmobile, toboggan, and ice skate.

Heavy rainstorms across the Indiana flatlands have always been dangerous. Through the years they have overflowed riverbanks and caused severe floods. In 1884 Clara Barton launched the first Red Cross flood relief program in Evansville after floodwater soaked the river town. Since then, floods have destroyed the Lake Michigan shoreline and town streets along the Ohio River.

Rain and melting snow frequently fill the three rivers of Fort Wayne. In March 1982 they spilled over, causing one of the state's worst floods ever. Over 50,000 volunteers, including schoolchildren, stuffed and piled one million sandbags along eight miles of flood walls.

In July 2003 seven consecutive days of rain caused the White River to overflow its banks and flood the town of Noblesville.

The sight of so many children coming together captured the nation's attention. Reporters called the heroic teamwork the "children's crusade."

PRESERVING THE BEST OF INDIANA

Indiana has a long history of citizens working together to better the environment. They want a state where people can be healthy and safe and where plants and animals from the region can continue to thrive for generations to come.

The Real Johnny Appleseed

One Indiana man who loved the earth was Massachusetts-born John Chapman. In about 1800 Chapman decided that "fruit is next to religion." He traveled westward from Massachusetts carrying a flour sack filled with apple, plum, and cherry seeds. Along the way the shoeless man with a tin pot for a hat planted his fruit seeds and preached. Orchards eventually bloomed wherever he hiked, earning Chapman the nickname Johnny Appleseed.

From 1838 until his death in 1845, Chapman wandered throughout Indiana. He planted one of his biggest orchards in Fort Wayne. Today, Chapman's grave site near Fort Wayne is named Johnny Appleseed Memorial Park. Every September people gratefully remember him with a festival bearing his name.

Saving the Dunes

In 1916 there was a great uproar over land. State lawmakers threatened to sell dune property for industrial development. Citizens fought back with the "Save the Dunes" movement. Seven years later the state bought the lakefront land for a park. Even so, a harbor was developed and land was chipped away for factories. The dunes weren't completely safe until 1971, when the state government created the Dunes Nature Preserve.

One woman, writer Juliet Strauss, led a campaign to save the forest at Turkey Run. Strauss learned in late 1915 that a timber company had bought the sweeping forest near her Rockville home and planned to cut down the trees. "Who would have dreamed a few men's dollars could step in and destroy . . . the most beautiful spot in Indiana," she said.

Strauss dashed off a letter to Indiana governor Samuel Ralston. Within a week Ralston appointed Strauss to a committee to save the forest. Strauss wrote biting articles about "timber wolves" in her regular *Indianapolis News* column, "The Country Contributor." Her persuasive attacks inspired the community to collect $40,000 to buy the land from the timber firm. Strauss is honored with a statue and a display recounting her good work at Turkey Run State Park.

More recently, local lawmakers created programs to protect the air, water, and land from pollution. In a report compiled in 2000 by *BioCycle* magazine, Indiana residents threw away 6.1 million tons of garbage. That's equal to the weight of 725,000 adult elephants! Like other states, Indiana is running out of places to dump its garbage. Legislators passed laws that would cut the amount of waste. The plan called for statewide programs to teach the public to "reduce and recycle" waste and to compost yard debris. Nine hundred government workers were hired to measure pollution and to develop teaching and recycling programs statewide.

"What we do for the environment is education through tours and park exhibits," says Randy Reed, a Turkey Run State Park ranger. "We show people a tiny piece of what Indiana looked like before people came."

Local corporations have pitched in by accepting recycled items. They have studied ways to use the throwaways in products they sell.

Indiana reduces pollution by offering rewards to industries that focus on protecting the environment.

Cities like Muncie require recycling of paper and metals that can be sold as raw materials for new goods. Muncie students participate by taking plastic bags, plastic six-pack rings, and laser printer cartridges to school. Schools give the waste products to recycling companies that donate money back to the schools in exchange for the students's work.

A main focus of Indiana environment programs is on protecting food, water, shelter, and space for animals and plants to thrive. Indiana, like other states, keeps a list of endangered or threatened wildlife. More than 150 fish, birds, reptiles, and animals that once prospered are in danger of disappearing from the state. Several programs have been created to either ensure that they last or to reintroduce specific species back into the state.

The Bald Eagle Reintroduction Program was the first endangered species restoration project in Indiana. In the early 1900s many bald eagles nested in Indiana. The introduction of pesticides by farmers to help their crops grow affected the bald eagles. By the 1980s bald eagles were about gone from Indiana. Scientists knew that bald eagle chicks returned to within fifty to one hundred miles of where they grew up. Between 1985 and 1989, the Bald Eagle Reintroduction Program released seventy-three chicks along Lake Monroe. By 2002 successful nests had grown from two in Monroe County to forty-five in a four-county area!

A similar project began to provide homes for barn owls. Places for them to nest in wooden barns and dead trees were disappearing. The government worked with private landowners to install nest boxes in new barns. To date, more than 320 barn owl nest boxes have been placed throughout southern Indiana.

Hoosiers believe that citizen education plays a key role in improving the environment for all living creatures. Wolf Park, in West Lafayette, created Howl Night to remind people to safeguard the environment for animals.

Less farm land and rapid development has reduced the barn owl population. Conservationist are working to increase their numbers.

Visitors can actually see packs of wolves mingling with bison in seminatural park settings. They can also learn different wolf calls and howl at the wolves, then wait to hear the wolves' answer.

Groups of concerned Indiana citizens continue to watch over their environment. From Yellowwood State Forest to the Calumet region, people carefully observe factory growth, logging, and road and building development. They are working hard to preserve habitats for wildlife and the natural beauty of their state.

Chapter Two

History Trail

I catch my breath as children do
In woodland swings when life is new . . .
When buds of Spring begin to blow
In blossoms that we used to know,
And lure us back along the ways
Of time's all-golden yesterdays!
—James Whitcomb Riley, "The All Golden"

James Whitcomb Riley was Indiana's most popular poet in the early 1900s. His poems recalled a state free of big-city differences and a place where people embraced similar ideas. His "people's poetry" described neighbors who were friendly and proud, and who shared a common past. Yet Riley overlooked much of what makes Indiana history so exciting—the joys and clashes of its many different voices.

EARLY SETTLEMENT

Native hunters were the first people who roamed the region about ten thousand years ago. They followed waterways in search of bison, elk, and

Karl Bodmer, a Swiss-born artist, captured the landscape of early New Harmony in New Harmony on the Wabash.

deer. These early wanderers left no written records, but archaeologists have uncovered animal and human bones, shells, and stone tools—clues to the simple migrant life the earliest humans in the area lived.

Prehistoric people who came after the hunters settled along the rivers. From about 1000 BCE to 1500 CE, they developed small farm communities and grew squash, pumpkins, and other seed plants. They carved stone tools, molded clay pots, and carried mud from the riverbeds to build large earth mounds to bury their dead. Historians named these people Mound Builders.

Later Mound Builders learned to plant corn and to hunt with bows and arrows. Their flat-topped mounds were centers of grand ceremonies in addition to being burial grounds. The mounds, many of which can still be seen today, were scattered over much of Indiana.

"At Angel Mounds, we have one of the best-preserved ancient Indian settlements in the United States," said Rodney Richardson of Angel Mounds.

Angel Mounds has eleven of these earthworks along the Ohio River. The tallest has three terraces and is forty-four feet high. Its 650-foot-long stockade wall is the largest prehistoric structure in the eastern United States.

Historians believe that Angel Mounds served as a capital for many nearby smaller settlements. At its peak, about three thousand people lived in the village. By 1450, however, the settlement was empty. Some scientists think the inhabitants ran out of food and died. Others think they disbanded and became the ancestors of later Native American nations.

MOVING WEST

Smaller groups of native corn farmers dotted Indiana country for the next two hundred years. Then waves of Miami, Potawatomi, and Kickapoo tribes migrated southward from the Great Lakes region. They were searching for better soil to farm and longer growing seasons. Other Indian nations joined them to hunt, fish, and farm. The Delaware, Munsee, and Shawnee fled from the east after European settlers forced them off their traditional lands.

French fur trader René-Robert Cavelier, Sieur de La Salle, was the first known European to scout Indiana. In 1679 he reached the "south bend" of the Saint Joseph River, where present-day South Bend lies. "Those lands surpass all others in everything," he wrote eagerly to the king of France.

The following year La Salle returned to learn more about northern Indiana. Other French fur traders

French explorer and fur trader René-Robert Cavelier, Sieur de La Salle, discovered the Ohio River in 1670 and was the first European to enter what is now Scott County.

brought blankets, whiskey, jewelry, tools, and weapons to swap for skins with the Indians. Trappers, missionaries, and explorers followed. By 1732 the French had built three trading posts along the Wabash River: Fort Ouiatenon (near present-day Lafayette), Fort Miami (now Fort Wayne), and the city of Vincennes. The French mingled with native tribes and tried to trade fairly. They hoped to secure Native American trade routes from Lake Erie to the Mississippi River.

Within a few years the British appeared and competed with the French for control of the profitable fur trade. Fighting between the two countries broke out during the 1750s. Native Americans saw that, wherever

Native Americans at the death of Louis-Joseph de Montcalm, commander of the French army in North America, during the French and Indian War

they settled, the British took over and treated the original people poorly. Many Indian tribes sided with France in what became the French and Indian War. By the time the battles ended in 1763, France had lost all lands west of the colonies.

Native Americans refused to admit defeat, however. Ottawa chief Pontiac gathered the Seneca, Ojibwa, Potawatomi, and other neighboring tribes to drive the British from the Great Lakes region. Pontiac's forces swept through Fort Ouiatenon and destroyed Fort Miami. Soldiers finally stopped them at Fort Detroit, at least for a while.

In 1775 another war erupted. This time the colonists fought to free themselves from British rule. Most fighting during the Revolutionary War took place in the east, but George Rogers Clark, who had moved from Virginia, pleaded for an army to help settlers fight the British in the west. "If a country is not worth protecting," he argued, "it is not worth claiming."

Clark's army won two major battles at Vincennes. His troops cut off British soldiers who had attacked the colonists from the west. Clark's successes helped change the course of the war. Soon after, the colonists were free to form an independent nation.

In 1779 George Rogers Clark conquered the British-held Fort Sackville near Vincennnes.

Present-day Indiana, Illinois, Ohio, Wisconsin, Michigan, and part of Minnesota became the Northwest Territory in 1787. Stories spread about the fertile, unpopulated region to the west. Wagon trains of pioneers who were tired of crowded towns in the eastern states set out to seek their fortunes. Settlers from Virginia and Kentucky paddled boats along the Ohio River.

"The emigrants who settled in Indiana at an early date came over the trails made by the Indians," wrote Colonel William Cockrun in 1907. "[They found] nothing but what they could manufacture and devise. . . . They had the great book of nature before them and were happy studying its changing scenes."

Pioneer life in Indiana was difficult. After crossing swamps, marshes, and rivers, families experienced the difficult task of felling trees and building cabins.

This flood of settlers horrified Native Americans. The Miami, Shawnee, Wea, and Delaware formed raiding parties to scare invaders off the land. Miami chief Little Turtle led the most crushing blows against the troops called in to protect the settlers in the Wabash Valley.

General Anthony Wayne's soldiers struck back at the Battle of Fallen Timbers on August 20, 1794. Wayne and his troops surrounded Little Turtle's army along the Maumee River, near present-day Toledo, Ohio, and kept charging until the Indians fled into the woods.

After the battle, Wayne's troops headed north along the river. They plundered Indian crops and destroyed villages until they reached the place where the Saint Marys and Saint Joseph rivers meet in Indiana. Here, General Wayne built a fort and named it after himself.

Little Turtle and his people were heartsick at the sweeping ruin Wayne had left behind. "The Americans are now led by a chief who never sleeps," Little Turtle said of his enemy.

New troops arrived to guard the forts. Indian raids stopped for the next fifteen years. By 1803 Ohio gained statehood. The remaining land in the Northwest Territory became the Indiana Territory, named for the Indian peoples who soldiers had tried to destroy.

FROM TERRITORY TO STATE

President Thomas Jefferson chose William Henry Harrison as territorial governor and Vincennes as headquarters. Jefferson ordered Harrison to protect settlers from unfriendly Indians. Harrison determined to silence the Indians forever by forcing them to move and buying their land along the Ohio River.

"Sell a country?" raged Shawnee chief Tecumseh. "Why not sell the air, the clouds, and the great sea as well as the earth?"

In 1810 Tecumseh resolved to unite the territory's tribes. He and his brother Tenskwatawa, the Prophet, gave fiery speeches against the sale of land to European settlers. Tecumseh charged that Indiana lands were "common property of the tribes and no one tribe had the right to cede [give up] land without consent of all."

Tecumseh's outraged supporters formed Prophetstown, a village along the Tippecanoe River. In 1811 Harrison countered by raising an army and building Fort Harrison nearby. The fort became a target for attacks from Prophetstown.

Tecumseh.

Tecumseh is best known as the Shawnee leader who attempted to protect native lands.

Harrison used the attacks as an excuse to invade the village, although he waited until Tecumseh was away. On a rainy November 7, 1811, Harrison's forces and the Prophet's followers clashed in the night. Each suffered heavy losses at the Battle of Tippecanoe. By daylight, the Prophet ordered his people to flee as Harrison destroyed their village. The town of Battle Ground was later built upon the site.

After the attack Tecumseh rushed from tribe to tribe rallying warriors. For almost two years his followers killed and kidnapped settlers and burned their homes. On October 5, 1813, Tecumseh was killed in the Battle of the Thames.

Without their forceful leader, the Indians no longer attacked. Some Native Americans fled to Ohio and Detroit but later were forced west. Others retreated to their villages. Settlers and Indians continued to clash from time to time, but Native Americans had pretty much lost control of the Wabash. A new era of settlement had begun.

Thirty years later Harrison would become the nation's ninth president. His campaign slogan referred to his days as an Indian fighter: "Tippecanoe and Tyler [his vice president] Too."

The attack of Native Americans at the Battle of Tippecanoe was a triumph for U.S. forces over Tecumseh's followers.

TIP AND TY

This song was written for the 1840 presidential campaign in which William Henry Harrison ran against Martin Van Buren. Harrison had been governor of Indiana when he led a victory over the Indians at the Tippecanoe River (near present-day Lafayette) in 1811. By 1840 he was known as "Old Tippecanoe" or simply "Tip."

Harrison won the election but died after only one month in office. Vice President John Tyler, know as "Ty," succeeded him.

Van.　Van is a | used - up man, And with them we'll beat lit - tle | Van.

Like the rushing of mighty waters,
    waters, waters,
On it I will go!
And in its course will clear the way
For Tippecanoe and Tyler too. *Chorus*

See the Loco standard tottering,
    tottering, tottering,
Down it must go!
And in its place we'll rear the flag
Of Tippecanoe and Tyler too. *Chorus*

Let them talk about hard cider, cider,
    cider,
And Log Cabins too,
It will only help to speed the ball
For Tippecanoe and Tyler too. *Chorus*

Don't you hear from every quarter,
    quarter, quarter,
Good news and true?
That swift the ball is rolling on
For Tippecanoe and Tyler too. *Chorus*

The Bay State boys turned out in
    thousands, thousands, thousands,
Not long ago,
And at Bunker Hill they set their seals
For Tippecanoe and Tyler too. *Chorus*

Have you heard from old Vermount,
    mount, mount,
All honest and true?
The Green Mountain boys are rolling the ball
For Tippecanoe and Tyler too. *Chorus*

His latchstring hangs outside the door,
    door, door,
And is never pulled through,
For it never was the custom of
Old Tippecanoe and Tyler too. *Chorus*

He always has his table set, set, set,
For all honest and true,
To ask you in to take a bite
With Tippecanoe and Tyler too. *Chorus*

Little Matty's days are numbered, numbered, numbered,
Out he must go!
And in his place we'll put the good
Old Tippecanoe and Tyler too. *Chorus*

KEE-BOON-MEIN-KAA POWWOW

In 2001 some 39,263 Indiana residents claimed Native American ancestry. These numbers represent 105 different tribes. To celebrate their heritage, Native Americans hold several ceremonies, or powwows, around the state every year. Powwows are like a family reunion, county fair, religious service, and sport's contest rolled into one event.

The Pokagon band of Potawatomi run the largest Indiana powwow in South Bend. About 12,000 people attend the Kee-boon-mein-kaa, meaning "We Quit Picking," to mark the end of huckleberry-picking season. The September ceremony begins with a grand entry parade at high noon, when the power of the sun, the creator, is greatest. A flag song follows, honoring U.S. and Canadian flags and the eagle staff, the pole with eagle feathers that represents warriors of old. A veteran's song honoring those who served in U.S. wars and a friendship dance call everyone together. The rest of the day is for dancing, displaying native beadwork and pottery, and feasting on fried bread, grape dumplings, and buffalo burgers.

A STATE COMES ALIVE

Before Fort Harrison was built, fewer than one thousand European settlers were scattered through the Indiana Territory. By 1813 wagonloads of pioneers streamed into the region. Almost 64,000 settlers made their homes in the Ohio Valley. Territorial government moved to a more central location in Corydon.

This early nineteenth-century engraving depicts the arrival of new settlers surging into Indiana with horse-drawn wagons loaded with farming tools.

Thomas Lincoln migrated with his family to southwest Indiana in 1816. He raised his famous son, Abraham, from ages seven to twenty-one in Spencer County. Then he relocated the family to Illinois. Abraham didn't think much of his log-cabin schooling in Indiana. "There was absolutely nothing to excite ambition for education," he recalled as president.

Indiana, meaning "Indian land," became the nineteenth state on December 11, 1816. As the state's population grew, so, too, did the need for more industry and, of course, land. Native Americans occupied the state's rustic northern two-thirds. The first elected governor, Jonathan Jennings, pressured the chiefs to sell land in middle Indiana.

This painting illustrates the surveyors who laid out the city of Indianapolis in 1823.

Then he sent commissioners to lay out a village in the heart of the state. By 1824 the governor was able to shift the state capital from Corydon to Indianapolis, its present site.

"The state treasurer moved state records in four oxcarts. The 125-mile trip took ten days," Corydon records affirmed.

Without the threats from Native Americans, the state's population exploded to almost 150,000 people. British and Scots-Irish pioneers from the south and east farmed and traded goods in central Indiana towns. Scandinavians farmed the eastern border, and German immigrants headed for the south. The *Indiana Gazette*, the state's first newspaper, attracted newcomers by printing, "No soil produces a greater abundance than that of Indiana."

CROSSROADS OF AMERICA

For the next twenty years, towns expanded near main water and land routes. Irish workers arrived to build canals and roads. Construction of the Wabash and Erie Canal in Wabash County opened the river to flatboat and steamboat traffic from the Great Lakes.

The *Florence*, the first steamboat to visit Terre Haute, arrived in about 1823. Fifteen years later, eight hundred steamers hauled grain, pork, and whiskey from bustling Indiana cities. The boats returned with more immigrants, who were attracted to land that sold for $1.25 an acre.

Indiana's stretches of the east-west National Road (now U.S. 40) and the north-south Michigan Road (now U.S. 421, Indiana routes 29 and 25, and U.S. 31) opened during the 1830s. These routes created direct overland links between the east and the west. Twelve stagecoach lines carted passengers through Indianapolis along the National Road. Many new roads connected the highways to smaller Indiana towns. Mines, quarries, mills, and factories sprang up near these routes, offering work for the newcomers.

"Most roads were only mud with deep ruts, water holes, and occasional rocks and boulders which made travel slow and difficult," remembered Otis Buckley of Geneva.

The National Road was the first federal highway in the United States. Its deeply rutted surface passed through Indianapolis.

In 1847 the first major Indiana railroad linked Madison and Indianapolis. Within three years railroad tracks in Indiana increased ten-fold, making steamboats outdated. Most cross-country railroad lines and highways passed through the state, earning Indiana its motto, "The Crossroads of America."

Sometime in the mid-1800s, Indiana residents adopted the nickname Hoosiers. No one knows for sure where the name originated. Many claim the word comes from the pioneer custom of greeting callers with "Who's yere?" One story links the name to workers of the canal builder Samuel Hoosier. Another legend traces *Hoosier* to the word *husher*, meaning "a strong riverboat worker," or to *hoozer*, a slang word for "hill dweller." Whatever the origin, the name stuck.

CIVIL WAR

Slavery was banned in Indiana upon statehood. By 1850 about 405 free African Americans lived in Indianapolis. Yet the state was still split over the issue of slavery. Many European settlers had come from southern states where it was common to own slaves. Such people tended to accept the cruel practice.

Other Hoosiers actively opposed slavery. Some opened their homes to runaway slaves as safe houses along the Underground Railroad, a secret path to freedom. One of the more traveled routes ran through eastern Indiana. Antislavery Quakers Levi and Catherine Coffin operated an important stop along this route in Fountain City. If runaways and those who helped them were captured, the punishments were beatings, jail, and even death. The Coffins dug an indoor well to hide the amount of water they used from outsiders. Many owners tracked their slaves to the Coffin house, only to find that the footprints had disappeared.

Thousands of runaway slaves seeking freedom arrived at Levi and Catherine Coffin's farm, a busy station of the Underground Railroad.

"There must be an Underground Railroad and Levi Coffin must be the president and his house the Grand Central Station," cried one angry slave owner. During their twenty years in Fountain City, Levi and Catherine Coffin helped two thousand runaways reach safety farther north.

The Civil War between the North and the South broke out in 1861. As a Northern state, Hoosiers fought on the side of the Union to keep the country united. Some Hoosiers who believed that slavery was okay resented the war. Still, nearly 210,000 Indiana men enlisted in the Union army, a larger number than from any other state besides New York. Only one battle was fought in Indiana, killing four guards. Overall, more than 24,000 Hoosiers died in service across the country— the greatest loss in Indiana military history.

Large numbers of African Americans migrated north after the Civil War. The strong-willed black minister John Clay worked tirelessly to bring his people from the South. "In Indiana all stand equal before the law. . . . Hitch up your teams and come overland," Clay, himself a former runaway slave, urged others.

By 1880 blacks totaled 15,931, or 9 percent, of the Indianapolis population, more than in other Indiana towns and most northern cities. But skilled jobs and many neighborhoods were still closed to blacks. That same year, however, James Hinton became the first African American elected to the state house of representatives.

"MAJOR" BICYCLE RIDER

In 1891 thirteen-year-old Marshall Taylor dressed in a military uniform to perform bicycle tricks. The "major" was to attract customers to the Hay & Willit bicycle store in Indianapolis. Mr. Hay, his boss, pushed young Taylor to ride in a race that his store sponsored. Taylor won against seasoned adults. Two years later, he broke the first of many speed records. He wanted to race more but was turned away. He was black.

To be allowed to race, Major had to move to Massachusetts. The move paid off. Major went on to become the fastest American short-distance bicycle racer. In 1899 he triumphed at a Montreal championship, making him the first black world racing superstar. One hundred years later, Indianapolis named a cycling track, the Major Taylor Velodrome, where bicyclers still race, in his honor.

Rapid industrial growth followed the Civil War. Plenty of coal, natural gas, stone, oil, and trees attracted varied industries to the state. The east-central region earned the name "gas belt" for its seemingly endless supply of natural gas. Glassmaking, which needed large amounts of gas, grew into a major state industry. With 110 plants, Indiana developed into the second-largest glass producer in the nation. Muncie became known as Glass Town for the Ball Corporation, a leading jar manufacturer.

Other industries led to the growth of towns. Bedford was called the "limestone capital of America" for its rich supply of high quality building rock. Sarah Breedlove (Madam C. J.) Walker employed hundreds of workers in her Indianapolis plants. Walker's hair-care products for African-American women made her the nation's first black and first female millionaire. By developing insulin, which controls life-threatening diabetes, Colonel Eli Lilly's company researchers produced this and other medicines that have saved countless lives.

During the late 1800s Hoosiers revolutionized transportation equipment. In 1894 Elwood Haynes of Kokomo built one of the first gas-run automobiles. Haynes remembered that during the test drive, his invention "moved off at a speed of about seven miles per hour and was driven about one and a half miles farther . . . without making a single stop." Observers called the machines such as the one Haynes manufactured "horseless carriages."

The Studebaker brothers owned the country's largest horse-drawn wagon factory in South Bend. Within ten years they had converted the company into a booming car industry. Major factory towns appeared in northern Indiana to support the expanding business. Oil refineries and steel mills transformed the small villages of Whiting, Hammond, Gary,

THE WALKER METHOD OF SUCCESS

Madam C. J. Walker, born Sarah Breedlove, was once a washer-woman in Vicksburg, Mississippi. After moving to Saint Louis, Missouri, she created a cream that made tight, curly hair easier to style. At first she mixed the oils and soaps in a washtub and sold the cream door-to-door.

Walker was so successful that in 1910 she built a factory in Indianapolis to manufacture her products. By then her Walker Method included shampoo, hair-growth pomade, vigorous brushing, and application with a heated metal comb. Walker also established a training center for her growing sales staff, the hallmark of her success. Walker offered inexperienced black women better pay and working conditions and, best of all, a job with dignity.

"I have made it possible for many colored women to abandon the washtub," she would say.

and East Chicago, places once known for their white pines and huckle-berries. Automobile-related industries continued to expand throughout the state well into the twentieth century.

Improved and expanded technology seemed to hurt Indiana farmers. Expensive steam-powered plows and threshers boosted production. Northern swamps around factory towns became farmland, glutting the market with surplus crops. As a result, crop prices fell, while the cost of harvesting increased. By 1900, 30 percent of Hoosier farmers were forced to sell their land and move to cities for better-paying jobs. For the first time, more Hoosiers earned their living in factories than on farms.

Factory workers often withstood terrible living and working conditions. Many toiled twelve hours a day six days a week for as little as fifteen cents an hour. Eugene Debs of Terre Haute achieved national acclaim as a "friend of the worker." Debs believed workers could change unfair labor practices by joining together in unions. He organized one of the first worker groups, the American Railway Union, during the 1890s.

Debs also argued for women's and children's rights. But his unpopular stands against factory owners and against Americans fighting in World War I landed him in jail. Refusing to give up, Debs took his pleas for fair

A 1904 campaign poster advertises Eugene Debs's run for the presidency under the Socialist Party, supporters of working-class America.

treatment of workers to the people. He ran for president five times as the candidate of the Socialist Party, including once from jail in 1920. That year he received almost a million votes!

"While there is a lower class I am in it," he declared. "While there is a soul in prison I am not free."

RISE AND FALL OF THE KLAN

Waves of African Americans from the South took jobs in the expanding steel mills and factories of Evansville, South Bend, and Gary. Thousands of immigrants from Poland, Hungary, Lithuania, Italy, and Mexico filled neighborhoods in the thriving towns of the Calumet region. Many longtime residents there believed that the newcomers were a threat to their well-being.

"Often bias in Indiana as elsewhere resulted from the fear of losing jobs," wrote Indiana historian John Bodnar.

During the 1920s Indiana became a stronghold of a national hate group, the Ku Klux Klan (KKK). White-hooded members of the Klan beat and bullied Catholics, Jews, and, especially, African Americans. The racist organization became so widespread that it sponsored women's clubs, children's contests, parades, and family outings. Individuals who opposed Klan ideas and its use of violence risked their businesses and lives, and the lives of family members.

In Indiana the Klan's most powerful leader was David Curtis Stephenson. Everyone in the state—the governor, mayors, judges, and local school boards—took orders from this Grand Dragon of hate. "I am the law and power in Indiana," warned Stephenson. Stephenson ruled the Klan until he was convicted of assaulting and killing Madge Oberholtzer. The Klan's popularity in Indiana then dwindled throughout the 1930s.

POPULATION GROWTH: 1810–2000

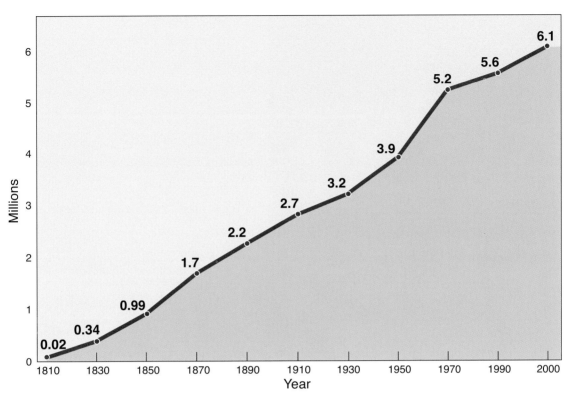

THE SPIRIT OF HOOSIERLAND

During World Wars I and II, Indiana ranked seventh in state output of war goods. Gunpowder, food for troops, and trucks went overseas. Existing factories were enlarged, and new plants were built to manufacture military products, attracting thousands of workers to the state.

Studebaker produced trucks that were sent to the Soviet Union. So many vehicles displayed the company name that Soviet soldiers thought *Studebaker* was English for *truck*.

During World War II, the Pullman-Standard plant in Hammond manufactured war equipment, such as field guns, shells, mortars, and tanks.

The decades following World War II were years of rapid growth in Indiana. As in the rest of the nation, cities were bursting at the seams. Suburbs overflowed onto flat farmlands. Interstate highways drew shoppers to malls far away from downtown areas. By the 1960s giant corporations began to close, too, leaving cities with high unemployment and decaying downtowns.

As a result, race riots erupted in many troubled cities around the country. Indiana towns, however, rarely faced this threat of racial violence. In 1967 Gary voters elected Richard Hatcher as mayor, one of the first African-American leaders of a major city in the United States.

Still, serious differences persisted in income and housing between black and white Hoosiers. To close the gap between rich and poor, many towns began programs to turn the economy around for all Hoosiers. The late 1980s and early 1990s were periods of renewal in which the state sought to enliven city centers and attract new industries. Historic landmarks received face-lifts. Large cities, like Indianapolis, built stadiums, museums, and parks to draw Hoosiers and out-of-staters alike.

Not all towns experienced improvements. Downtown Indianapolis and Terre Haute bustled with new construction. In towns like Kentland

Soldiers' and Sailors' Monument in Indianapolis, completed in 1901, is dedicated to the heroes of Indiana who died in wars prior to World War I. The monument was renovated in 1989.

and New Middletown, however, empty factories and run-down homes remained as ghostly reminders of the vanished businesses.

In the late 1990s the entire country experienced an economic downturn. Cash-strapped Indiana suffered with layoffs, job losses, and increased class sizes in schools. The state was bleeding workers who followed jobs elsewhere. Government feared a huge talent drain in all areas. In 1999 the state began offering grants in education, science, and technology in an effort to keep jobs and workers in state. Still, without federal government support, Indiana continues to lose jobs, workers, and tax money to run local programs.

In spite of many changes and problems, Indiana cities have kept their small-town feeling. Hoosiers retain the ability to relax, even in the midst of economic downturns or fast-paced city life. As Irving Liebowitz wrote in the Pulitzer Prize-winning *My Indiana:*

Generally speaking, Hoosiers have learned the value of the simple things in life. They are in no great rush and are not overawed by wealth, position or prestige [fame]. Hoosiers may live in the present and plan for the future, but they jealously guard the past.

Down-Home Hoosiers

"Y'all have a nice day," calls a Corydon Hoosier with a southern drawl. "I work in *de* region," explains one Calumet worker.

The way many Hoosiers talk is a clue to where they live in the state. Generally, the farther north in Indiana, the more *th* becomes *d* and a midwestern big-city twang appears. Central Hoosiers add an *r* to some words, saying *Worshington* instead of *Washington*. South of Bloomington, people have the southern drawl of their ancestors, who may have come from Kentucky or Virginia.

With sizable Hispanic populations in the Calumet region, Koreans in Muncie, and Japanese in Lafayette, the state blends speech patterns from around the world. These are the many voices of Indiana. Add their folklore and traditions and you have the heart and soul of Hoosierland—its everyday people.

SMALL-TOWN FOLK

"Northwest Indiana is big enough to be interesting and little enough where everyone knows everyone else," says Indiana University student Katherine Belcher.

Hoosier pride is reflected by an outpouring of community spirit for high school and college sports.

In 2004 the U.S. Census Bureau assessed Indiana as having about 6.2 million people. This figure ranks fourteenth among the fifty states. After years of decline, the state's population is finally making a small but sure comeback. During the 1980s thousands of young adults left the state. As the economy recovered during the late 1990s, however, more returned than moved away.

Three of every four Hoosiers born in Indiana stay for life. As a result, Indiana's population recently has increased by 9.7 percent. Into the twenty-first century, Indiana is attracting more residents than it looses for the first time in years.

Even with such gains, most of Indiana provides a livable blend of elbow room and neighbors. An average of only about 170 people occupy a square mile. Like the rest of the nation, much of Indiana's growth has occurred in the suburbs, but few Hoosier cities are bursting at the seams. Instead, the state contains about sixteen scattered population centers of at least 35,000 people each. Most of those are county seats, each with a fancy courthouse, proud war memorial, and local government buildings. About one-third of Hoosiers live in towns with fewer than two thousand people.

"People are sick of huge cities," observes one resident. "My whole family moved to Brown County from San Diego, California."

The largest city is the state capital, Indianapolis. About 26 percent of Hoosiers live in Indianapolis and its surrounding suburbs. Hoosiers like to call the eight counties circling the center city "doughnut" counties. With about 1.6 million people, this metropolitan area represents a continually growing share of the state's population. Fort Wayne, with a population of 219,000, and Evansville, with 117,000, are the state's next largest urban areas. Cities of the Calumet region, which are linked by the Calumet River, blend into one bustling population center.

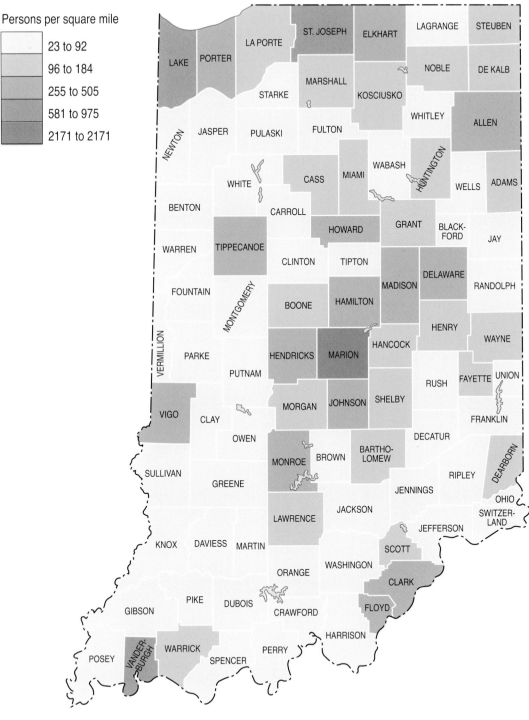

Persons per square mile

23 to 92

96 to 184

255 to 505

581 to 975

2171 to 2171

LAKE
PORTER
LA PORTE
ST. JOSEPH
ELKHART
LAGRANGE
STEUBEN
NOBLE
DE KALB
MARSHALL
STARKE
KOSCIUSKO
WHITLEY
ALLEN
NEWTON
JASPER
PULASKI
FULTON
WHITE
CASS
MIAMI
WABASH
HUNTINGTON
WELLS
ADAMS
BENTON
CARROLL
HOWARD
GRANT
BLACK-FORD
JAY
WARREN
TIPPECANOE
CLINTON
TIPTON
MADISON
DELAWARE
RANDOLPH
FOUNTAIN
MONTGOMERY
BOONE
HAMILTON
HENRY
WAYNE
VERMILLION
PARKE
PUTNAM
HENDRICKS
MARION
HANCOCK
RUSH
FAYETTE
UNION
VIGO
CLAY
OWEN
MORGAN
JOHNSON
SHELBY
FRANKLIN
DECATUR
SULLIVAN
GREENE
MONROE
BROWN
BARTHO-LOMEW
RIPLEY
DEARBORN
JENNINGS
OHIO
JACKSON
SWITZER-LAND
LAWRENCE
JEFFERSON
KNOX
DAVIESS
MARTIN
SCOTT
WASHINGON
CLARK
ORANGE
GIBSON
PIKE
DUBOIS
CRAWFORD
FLOYD
HARRISON
POSEY
VANDER-BURGH
WARRICK
SPENCER
PERRY

POPULATION DENSITY

ETHNIC INDIANA

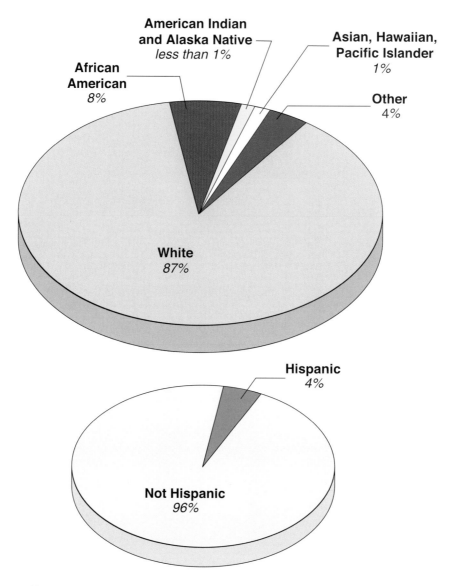

American Indian and Alaska Native *less than 1%*

Asian, Hawaiian, Pacific Islander *1%*

African American *8%*

Other *4%*

White *87%*

Hispanic *4%*

Not Hispanic *96%*

Note: A person of Cuban, Mexican, Puerto Rican, South or Central American, or other Spanish culture or origin regardless of race is defined as Hispanic.

"People think of Indiana as a white bread state," explained Robert Taylor of the Indiana Historical Society. "We always had diversity. It just wasn't as obvious."

Less than 13 percent of Indiana is nonwhite, mostly (8 percent) African American. But a Spanish-speaking population is growing quickly. Between 1990 and 2000 Indiana's Hispanic population increased by 116,000 people to 3.5 percent of the state's population. By 2003 the Hispanic population had risen to 4 percent. Most have settled near larger, more industrial areas in Marion, Lake, Elkhart, Allen, Saint Joseph, Tippecanoe, and Porter counties.

Ethnic diversity is on the rise in Indiana with minority groups representing a small but growing segment of the state's population.

More than half of Hispanic people in the United States speak Spanish only. Schools and local and state governments grapple with how best to serve people who know a language other than English. Should children be taught in Spanish or English in school? Should instructions on forms and labels in public places be written in both languages? Long ago, the state attracted large numbers of residents of German, Scots-Irish, English, and French descent. But now, Hispanics in Indiana outnumber all other groups that speak another language besides English.

Pockets of Hoosiers still refuse to accept diversity. "Some people are blatant in racism," charges a Brown County resident. "I had a man spit in my face in the street because I was walking with a black friend."

Some southern Indiana towns have bad reputations among minorities. Small groups of the Ku Klux Klan still try to recruit members to their racist organization. A few times each year they burn crosses on front lawns, a reminder of a time when the Klan controlled Indiana.

Larger numbers of Hoosiers, however, strive for racial understanding. The Indiana Humanities Council selects different cultures for communities to highlight. From 1996 to 1999 Hoosiers explored their growing trade relationships with Asian countries. Asian fairs, videos, and lectures gave Hoosiers greater understanding of their neighbors from other lands.

In 1999 the council launched a program to connect Indiana with its German roots. According to the 1990 census, one in three Hoosiers claimed German ancestry. The council arranged several sister-city projects with Germany, including Web site links and public programs and projects to help Hoosiers learn about German culture and how it compares with life in Indiana.

Every fall since 1984 Columbus has spotlighted different cultures with a grand ethnic exposition. Almost 35,000 visitors enjoy three days of ethnic foods, street dances, an international bazaar, and art displays. A treat for the entire family is the colorful kite fly.

"Kids make kites at the expo and fly them the next day at Clifty Park," explains organizer Debra Lee. "We all fly together around the world."

DIFFERENT FAITHS

Religion in Indiana mirrors the state's ethnic mix. Roman Catholics maintain sizable Hoosier congregations. Smaller numbers of Indiana worshippers are members of the Protestant, Islamic, and Jewish faiths. On the road leading west into Bloomington, a large Jewish center stands next to Baptist and Lutheran churches. So many churches and

In Indiana there are a variety of observed religions. This diversity includes Sikhs and Buddhists, as well as Catholics, Protestants, and Jews.

temples representing different beliefs line Hammond's Hohman Avenue that the street is known as Church Row.

During the 1800s several religious communities came to Indiana seeking safe places to pray. Among the earliest groups were the Harmonists. In 1814 German religious leader George Rapp bought 30,000 acres of southwest Indiana forest for his Harmonie Society. The peaceful Harmonists farmed, established mills and factories, and constructed 180 buildings. They named their successful town Harmonie.

Social reformer Robert Owen and his financial partner William Maclure bought Harmonie in 1825 and changed its name to New Harmony. Owen dreamed of a community that would "unite all interests into one." More than eight hundred scientists, scholars, and educators helped Owen create a learning center on the frontier.

The experiment in equality failed after three years. Still, Owen and Maclure pioneered many advances in equal rights and education, especially for women. Harmonist Fanny Wright boldly challenged the thinking of the time that women were unequal to men, something women had never dared to express in public. Her speeches were thought to be so shocking that men insultingly called women "Fanny Wrightists."

Moravians founded the historic community of Hope in 1830 as part of their church's plan to expand along the frontier. The old Moravian Cemetery remains unchanged. Rows of limestone markers lie flat on the ground as a symbol of the Moravian belief that all people are equal in death.

The Amish, a strict Mennonite sect, established farms outside Berne, in northeast Indiana, and in Daviess County. The Amish obey the Bible's warning to "be not conformed to this world." Members live very simply in farming communities. They forgo modern comforts like cars and electricity, dress in plain clothes, grow their own foods, and make tools and furniture by hand.

The Amish can trace their religious beliefs back to Switzerland in the sixteenth century.

Men dress in mostly handmade, dark-colored hats and pants. Women wear long dark dresses and bonnets. Most Amish children ride to one-room schoolhouses in horse-drawn buggies. A visit through Amish country is a journey into an earlier time.

BOOK LEARNING

Hoosiers claim many firsts in education. In 1816 lawmakers wrote the first state constitution that required free public education. New Harmony freethinkers introduced the nation to preschools, adult trade schools, and the idea of free public libraries. Harmonists offered some of the first public classes in which boys and girls studied together.

Even with these strong beginnings, Indiana was slow to provide equal education for all races. Black and white children would not go to the same schools for a long time. Usually, black schools received less funds and were poorly staffed. An exception was an African-American high school called Crispus Attucks, which opened in 1927. Attucks students traveled from the far corners of Indianapolis to attend classes. They were taught by an all-black faculty that included some of the best minds in the United States. Many talented black scholars taught high school instead of pursuing other careers because their skin color kept them from rising in their chosen fields.

"As a result, students received an excellent education from a stable staff," notes Gilbert Taylor of the Crispus Attucks Center. "We have graduates in all walks of life now. Our alumni hold important jobs around the world in sizable numbers."

Indiana schools kept white and black students apart until a 1949 state law banned segregated public education. Even then, separate schools persisted in some areas for decades. Not until 1982 did statewide integrated education become a reality. To achieve racial balance, many of Attucks's more experienced teachers transferred to other schools. Now the school is an African-American learning center and museum within the Indianapolis school district. Gallery exhibits depict events in African-American history. The center also houses the state's high school basketball hall of fame.

Today, every Indiana child from age six to sixteen must attend school. As in many states, however, some districts turn out better-educated students than others. One in ten students enrolls in private school, partly to get a better education.

"We think our schools and teachers are very good," observes a Noblesville public school teacher. "We find that kids who move here from other districts are always behind."

Indiana's Department of Education has set goals for its students so they may achieve academic success in language arts, mathematics, social studies, and science.

To improve education statewide, teachers developed ISTEP (Indiana Statewide Testing for Education Programs) in 1988. Hoosier students take ISTEP tests to learn which areas, if any, they need to improve. Another law, passed in 1995, attempts to reduce the number of students who drop out before high school graduation. Usually, Hoosier teens may drive at age sixteen. But students who quit school early or skip too many classes must wait until their eighteenth birthday to apply for a driver's license.

A newer plan to upgrade Indiana education is the Twenty-first Century Community Learning Centers Program. Part of their work involves Community Learning Centers, after-school programs for children in rural and inner-city areas. Activities are geared to enrich opportunities for children who attend low-performing schools or schools in poor areas. In 2002 about 6,800 rural and inner-city public schools in 1,420 communities joined with local businesses and organizations to enhance learning experiences for their students through this program.

Hoosiers are proud of the state's more than forty public and private colleges and universities. David Letterman, late-night talk show host, once boasted about his great education from Ball State University in Muncie. He liked it so much that the wacky Hoosier comic funds a scholarship there for C students.

The largest state-run institution, Indiana University, has eight campuses statewide. The main campus, with 30,000 students, stretches for miles in Bloomington. Its many grand buildings house some of the finest university programs in the nation, particularly in music, law, and business. The university's Indianapolis campus houses the second-largest medical school in the country.

Young graduates celebrate at their commencement ceremony at the University of Indiana.

Purdue University's main campus, in Lafayette, has the largest international student body in the state. The school excels in agricultural research, engineering, and, particularly, computer science. Another distinguished area of research for the college is the aerospace industry.

Amelia Earhart, the first woman pilot to fly across the Atlantic Ocean, was a consultant in the Department of the Study of Careers for Women at Purdue. In 1929 she founded a group called the 99s, whose members included 99 of the 117 women pilots in the country. Today the 99s is an international organization of about six thousand women. Purdue houses the largest collection of Earhart materials, including photos she took on her many flights and Coast Guard logs of the vain search to locate her lost plane.

Purdue's aerospace school has been nicknamed "mother of astronauts." Among its famous graduates is Mitchell-born Virgil Grissom, the first person to travel on two space flights. Neil Armstrong, another Purdue-trained astronaut, made the universally acclaimed first walk on the moon in July 1969. In 1984 alone, Purdue claimed seven astronauts trained for space travel.

Purdue has a mission to bring learning into communities. The university hires educators to work in every county of the state, presenting workshops about topics that affect Hoosiers. Educators form 4-H programs for boys and girls to develop leadership skills for the future. These teachers are even involved in planning the Indiana State Fair. As one Hoosier wrote, "The entire state has long been the Purdue University campus."

Surprisingly, Notre Dame, a private Catholic university known for its winning football team, has become a center for Mexican-American studies. Julian Samora had suffered many racial insults as a Mexican-American boy in southern Colorado. He vowed to combat prejudice with knowledge. While at Notre Dame, Professor Samora helped found the National Council of La Raza, a leading civil rights organization. He pioneered research on Mexican Americans in the Midwest. After Samora's death in 1996, Notre Dame created the Julian Samora Research Institute to expand his work on behalf of Mexican Americans.

FRIED BISCUITS

"Everything is fried in Indiana," says a shopkeeper, shaking her head.

Indiana is the land of biscuits and gravy, fried chicken, and country-fried steaks. And everything here is fried, even the biscuits. Ask an adult to help you make this popular Hoosier recipe.

1/3 package dry yeast
2 cups milk
1/8 cup sugar
1/4 cup vegetable oil
2 teaspoons salt
3 1/2 to 4 1/2 cups flour

Add the yeast to warm water according to packet directions. Add the other ingredients and let the dough stand until it puffs up, or rises. Pat the dough down and form into separate biscuits. Drop them into hot oil, which should cover the bottom of the frying pan. Fry on both sides until golden brown.

Indiana has a rich network of history buffs. Some work for the library system, but many are volunteers, including young historians. They publish and distribute information and support local historical societies and libraries.

In 1938 the Indiana Junior Historical Society was founded, and it is going strong today. Boys and girls from fourth grade through high school learn pioneer crafts, visit historic sites, and discover ways to conserve Indiana's past. Many go to summer history camp and the annual history convention. They learn about ancient digs and famous Hoosiers. Most of all, they learn that history can be fun.

Indiana's youth can enhance their knowledge of their state's history by visiting local libraries, museums, and education centers throughout the state.

Chapter Four

Running Hoosierland

"Yes, the old state . . . has struck a right good average," said Indiana-born vice president (and former governor of the state) Thomas Marshall in 1913. "It has surely furnished as many first-grade second-class men in every department of life as any state in the Union."

During the 1920s Robert and Helen Merrell Lynd studied Muncie, Indiana, as a "typical American community." These sociologists published reports in 1929 and 1937 hailing Muncie as "Middletown," a place where average Americans were practical and independent. Soon all Hoosiers were said to display these "down-home" traits in the way they lived and governed.

INSIDE GOVERNMENT

Hoosiers manage the most productive state government in the Midwest, though Indiana receives the fewest federal dollars of all fifty states. Yet the state has low taxes and a smaller public workforce than any other state in the Midwest. The trade-off is that citizens receive fewer public services, such as sick pay, school improvements, and public housing. Parents even have to rent their children's textbooks.

Indiana's State House is home to all three branches of the government, as well as the governor's office, the General Assembly, and the State Supreme Court.

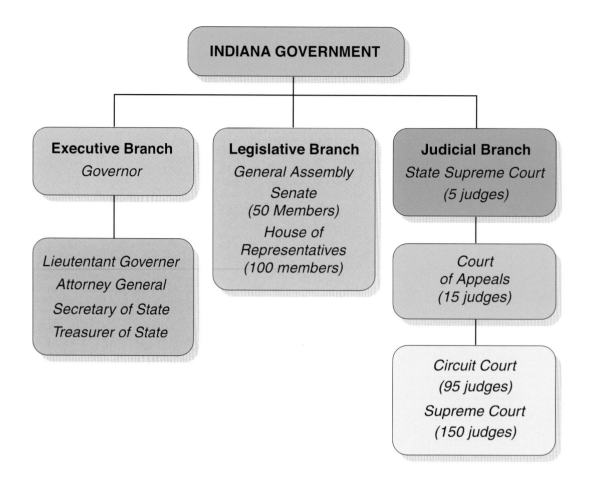

INDIANA GOVERNMENT

Executive Branch
Governor

Lieutentant Governer
Attorney General
Secretary of State
Treasurer of State

Legislative Branch
General Assembly
Senate
(50 Members)
House of
Representatives
(100 members)

Judicial Branch
State Supreme Court
(5 judges)

Court
of Appeals
(15 judges)

Circuit Court
(95 judges)
Supreme Court
(150 judges)

Indiana government is divided into three separate branches: executive, legislative, and judicial. As in the federal government, the branches check one another in making, interpreting, and carrying out the laws.

Executive

The state's chief executive officer is the governor. Every four years Hoosiers choose a governor. The governor's tasks are to appoint state workers, sign or veto (reject) bills, command the state military, and oversee seven elected officers who run various state agencies.

In 1988 Evan Bayh won the Democratic Party its first governor's office in twenty-four years. Bayh was only thirty-two years old, young for such an important position. Four years later voters reelected Bayh by the widest vote of any Hoosier governor in the twentieth century. He was especially popular with women voters, who were pleased to see more females heading important agencies during his administration than in most other states. He was elected to the U.S. Senate in 1998 and again in 2004.

Another popular leader, Frank O'Bannon, came to office on the coattails of Evan Bayh. But Governor O'Bannon entered office during difficult times. Although reelected for a second term and much loved around the state, he suffered from the same economic downturn that battered the rest of the nation. Critics worried that the state had lost too many farm and industry jobs. They tried to blame O'Bannon for the shrinking state budget and reduced services. He died in office in 2003. The office of governor was filled by Joseph Kernan, O'Bannon's lieutenant governor. In the 2004 election for governor, Mitch Daniels won 52 percent of the vote against incumbent Governor Joseph Kernan, becoming Indiana's forty-ninth governor.

Mitch Daniels won Indiana's 2004 gubernatorial election.

Indiana's two-chamber legislature is called the General Assembly. The fifty members in the senate are elected for four years. The one hundred elected members of the house of representatives serve for two-year terms. Hoosier legislators tend to stay in office for several terms, longer than in most other states. "We have the best legislature money can buy" is an old joke heard in the statehouse.

A key legislative job is to make laws. A majority of all members in each chamber must approve a bill before it can become law. Then the bill goes to the governor, who either signs the bill into law or vetoes it. Even if the governor rejects a bill, it can still become law if a majority in both houses overrides the veto. Indiana is unusual in requiring only a majority

Indiana's General Assembly, the lawmaking body of the government, has been meeting in the State House since 1887.

of more than half the votes to override. Most other states require a two-thirds majority.

Some legislators have become known for the type of bills they propose. In 1972 Julia Carson became the first black woman to serve in the state house of representatives. She sponsored bills to benefit women and the poor, including a minimum-wage law for domestic workers. In 1996 Carson made history again as the first black woman to be elected to the U.S. Congress as a state representative. She was elected to her fifth term in 2004.

A key issue for the legislature has been the education of students past high school. Lawmakers wanted to offer families without enough money some ways to send their children to college. The Twenty-first Century Community Learning Centers Scholars Program was first introduced in 1990. Any seventh and eighth grader could enroll in the program and be guaranteed the cost of four years of in state college if they met state guidelines. Lawmakers updated the law every few years. In 1996 they voted to prepare a report of how well the program worked. A study found that 1.7 million Hoosiers have taken advantage of the program. Indiana went from fortieth in 1986 to seventeenth in 1998 in state rankings for numbers of students to attend college.

Julia Carson has dedicated her life to public service and "pledges to continue to help build a safe, caring, and responsible community."

The judicial branch interprets laws and hears cases against individuals or businesses. A five-member supreme court is the highest court in the state. These judges hear cases from the fifteen-judge court of appeals. This court receives cases from individuals who challenge results from lower courts. Judges from ninety circuit courts and many county and special courts hear cases closer to home.

LOCAL LOYALTIES

"I call the state of Indiana the state of confusion," says one Indianapolis teacher.

Indiana, like many other states, has a jumble of smaller, overlapping government districts. The state has 92 counties, 1,008 townships, 115 cities, and 460 towns. Ideally, local agencies cooperate to run schools, police, and highway construction. But it didn't always work that way.

In 1970 Mayor Richard Lugar pushed through a program to combine the resources of Indianapolis city with those of the surrounding county. City and Marion County governments formed "Unigov," short for "unified government." The plan enlarged Indianapolis to Marion County borders and decreased government agencies from sixty to six.

Before Unigov was formed, Indianapolis had been declared one of America's dirtiest cities. The new government tackled a major cleanup effort. Agencies worked together to clean urban areas and reduce crime. Within ten years Indianapolis turned around. Indianapolis is now one of the nation's cleanest cities with one of the lowest crime rates.

Counties were a form of local government before statehood and before larger population centers developed. Hoosiers continue to think of themselves as coming from a county. Most residents give travel directions by

Indianapolis, the state capital, is the largest city in the state.

**INDIANA
BY COUNTY**

county rather than by nearness to a city or a town. This can be confusing to visitors who are unfamiliar with Indiana county names and borders.

Indiana government has a history of farmers battling with city folk. Because local loyalties are stronger than anything else in Indiana, few Hoosiers have gained power beyond state borders. Only a small number of them have earned national government acclaim. William Henry Harrison, Indiana territorial governor, became president of the United States in 1841. But he died thirty-one days after taking office. His grandson Benjamin Harrison, the only other Hoosier president, served from 1889 until 1893.

Being second in command seems to suit Hoosiers better. The United States has had five vice presidents from Indiana: Schuyler Colfax (served 1869–1873), Thomas Hendricks (1885), Charles Fairbanks (1905–1909), Thomas Marshall (1913–1921), and J. Danforth Quayle (1989–1993). Hoosiers call the state the "mother of vice presidents."

Hailing from Indianapolis, Dan Quayle was vice president under President George Bush from 1989–1993.

Chapter Five

Hoosiers at Work

"Indianapolis, like other Indiana towns, does not depend on one industry. It's diversified, so the city doesn't shut down if one industry folds," noted one resident.

Hoosiers have seen the problems of running single-business towns. When the steel industry declined in the 1980s, 22,000 jobs were lost in Gary alone. Crime soared and unemployment skyrocketed as businesses left the city.

Therefore, towns—from Muncie and Terre Haute to Gary and Evansville—are seeking to produce a surprising variety of goods. Indiana may be small in size among the states, but it remains in the top ten for factory and farm output.

MANUFACTURING

Indiana ranks an amazing number one in the nation for manufacturing jobs. One in five nonfarm jobs comes from factory work. Of these, one in seven is linked directly to goods exported from the state out of the country. Almost half of Indiana products go to Canada, the state's leading

Eli Lilly, based in Indianapolis, is a leader in the pharmaceutical industry. This scientist is employed by Eli Lilly's research lab.

trade partner, and transportation equipment tops the list of products that are exported. Such Indiana industries as containers and steel have remained national leaders since the early 1900s.

The heart of Indiana manufacturing is still in the Calumet region, where steel is king. Even with major cutbacks, blast furnaces in Burns Harbor, East Chicago, and Gary remain the world's leading steel producers. Much of the steel goes into manufacturing transportation-related equipment.

Steel is one of Indiana's largest industries. A metal slab of steel exits the furnace at a mill in Kokomo (above).

Raw steel is shipped to factories throughout Indiana to produce parts for cars, trucks, and airplanes. The parts are then transported to assembly plants near Lafayette and Fort Wayne. More cargo trailers for trucks are produced by Wabash National Corporation at Lafayette than anywhere else in the United States.

Elkhart County, in northern Indiana, has been called the "recreational vehicle [RV] capital of the world." The trend began after the 1933 Chicago World's Fair, where Elkhart's Wilbur Schult looked over a vehicle made by trailer pioneer Ray Gilkison of Terre Haute. Schult determined to produce a better trailer and eventually did. His resolve made his company, and later Indiana, an industry leader.

By the 1960s three brothers from Elkhart had devised a way to modify trailers into comfortable yet affordable homes. They started Coachmen Industries, selling twelve mobile homes the first year. Today the company employs more than four thousand people in fourteen states and builds twelve homes a day and countless travel and camping trailers. Indiana produces almost 60 percent of all trailers and mobile homes in the United States. Over half of these come from Elkhart alone.

Elkhart's recreational vehicle industry provides one of every four jobs in the city and is responsible for more than $1 billion in annual salaries.

EARNING A LIVING

Manufacturing

- Chemicals
- Electrical & electronic products
- Food processing
- Machinery
- Steel
- Transportation

Agriculture

- Beef Cattle
- Corn
- Hogs
- Soybeans
- Tobacco
- Vegetables
- Wheat

Natural Resources

- Coal
- Forest products
- L Limestone
- Oil
- Sand, gravel

Lake Michigan

Hammond
Gary
South Bend
Elkhart
L

Kankakee R.
Fort Wayne

Tippecanoe R.
Logansport
Wabash R.
Huntington

West Lafayette
Lafayette
Kokomo
Marion
Mississinewa R.

Frankfort
Muncie

L
White R.
Anderson

Crawfordsville
Eel R.
Indianapolis
Richmond
Brookville Lake

Terre Haute
Greensburg

Wabash R.
Bloomington
Columbus
Monroe Lake
L

White R.
Bedford
Madison
Ohio R.

Vincennes
Shoals
New Albany

Patoka Lake

Evansville
Ohio R.

During the 1920s Elkhart was the "band instrument capital of the world," too. Elkhart gained fame for its clarinets, trombones, and flutes. Companies like Selmer expanded to sell wind, percussion, and string instruments. Today other states produce competing products. Elkhart, though, remains a top player in the musical instrument field.

Medical instruments, too, remain a strong manufacturing industry. Indiana University School of Medicine and Eli Lilly medicines help the industry stay alive in Indianapolis. Governor O'Bannon created the Twenty-First Century Research and Technology Fund to keep new ideas flowing into industry. Extra funding has helped Indiana companies continue to lead the nation in the production of medical instruments and supplies.

Overall, Indiana manufacturing took a nosedive from 2000 to 2003, as the nation's economy declined. Indiana lost more jobs than forty-eight out of fifty states, a situation that may continue for awhile.

AGRICULTURE

Farmland blankets about 70 percent of Hoosierland. Indiana's vast system of roads, railways, and waterways enables farmers to deliver crops easily to state, national, and international markets.

Corn and soybeans account for about half of Indiana's yearly farm income. Related corn products, such as popcorn and cerealine, make Hoosiers industry leaders. Cerealine, which comes from processing corn into cornstarch, was originally developed at Columbus in 1880. This ingredient became the basis of dry, flaked cereals. When it was introduced into the cereal market, cerealine started a new trend in breakfast foods.

Other important Hoosier crops are hay, oats, potatoes, and apples. Winter wheat covers much of central Indiana during cold weather. New Albany's tobacco market sells several million pounds of leaves each season.

A farmer inspects his crop of corn, one of Indiana's major cash crops.

Indiana ranks in the top ten among states in hog and chicken production. Regions around Lafayette and Vincennes are strongholds of the state's hog industry. Hoosier chickens provide more eggs than any state in the country besides California. And Colonel Harland Sanders, of Henryville, Indiana, created the hugely successful Kentucky Fried Chicken restaurant chain.

The recent national trend toward fewer but larger farms hit Indiana hard. From the mid-1980s until the 1990s, the number of farms dropped from 88,000 to 65,000. As a result, many family farmers sold their land and found factory jobs in nearby towns. The downward trend seems to be continuing.

THE POPCORN KING

Hoosier Orville Redenbacher experimented for twenty-four years at Purdue University to find "perfect popcorn that popped light and fluffy." In 1965 he developed a special popcorn called snowflake that expanded to twice the size of other varieties. His invention eventually made him famous throughout North America and Europe. He sold his company, though, before sales had really begun to take off.

Each September since 1979 thousands of people gather in Valparaiso to celebrate Redenbacher and local popcorn growers at the Popcorn Festival. The first festival and its twelve-foot-diameter popcorn ball made the *Guinness Book of Records*. Today visitors honor Redenbacher's success with popcorn teen dances, popcorn kernel races, a parade, and any number of popcorn treats, including popcorn lollipops.

Farming still lies at the heart of Indiana, though. For twelve days every August, farm-related activities are celebrated at the Indiana State Fair. Farm goods, homemade crafts, and farm equipment highlight the festive celebration. Families enjoy pig races, ballooning, fiddling contests, and a carnival.

Children compete in contests for the best-cared-for pig or rabbit or for the most original vegetable decoration. During the year local 4-H groups around the state prepare boys and girls for the contests. Once, 4-H programs included only livestock and home-making projects. Nowadays Indiana children can explore photography, computers, model making, sports, and more. In Dubois County, the 4-H slogan is "Learn by Doing."

INDIANA WORKFORCE

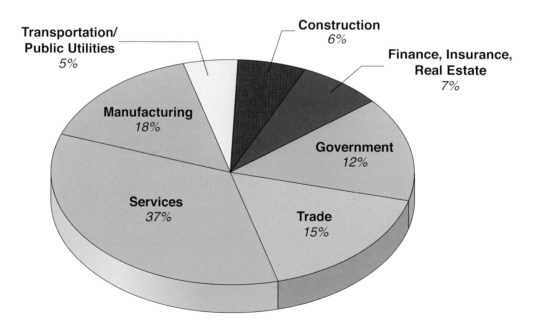

Construction
6%

Finance, Insurance,
Real Estate
7%

Transportation/
Public Utilities
5%

Manufacturing
18%

Government
12%

Services
37%

Trade
15%

Service industries, those jobs where people help people, account for an increasing proportion of Indiana jobs. One in four people sells, serves, or consults. Government makes up the major share of these jobs. But Hoosier transportation companies also hire large numbers of employees. Two of the nation's twenty biggest commercial carriers maintain headquarters in Indiana. About thirty railroads employ workers to help carry freight across the state.

Indiana tourism is a small but growing service industry. Sports events, like the Indianapolis 500, lure the most visitors. Local tourism revolves around community festivals and attractions. Even the smallest towns attract visitors with celebrations of town history, hometown heroes, and local products.

According to Indiana folklore, almost every Hoosier is a writer. In 1947 Purdue University librarian John Moriarity investigated whether Indiana

More than 200,000 fans attend the eighty-eighth Indianapolis 500.

really had more writers than other states. Moriarity happily discovered that Indiana ranked second only to New York State in the number of best-selling authors. (And New York had four times as many people!)

Today, one well-known writer who grew up in Indiana, Kurt Vonnegut Jr., likes to test Hoosier limits. Vonnegut writes about human problems, rather than Hoosier ideals. Vonnegut mocks the Middle America that most Hoosiers stand for. He makes fun of foul-smelling factories, self-important adults, religion, and gun-toting hunters who claim to be peace loving. The Indianapolis-born author lives in the East now.

Hoosier writers have always shown a sense of humor. The most famous modern Hoosier cartoon character is Garfield the cat. Cartoonist Jim Davis has been drawing the lasagna-eating lazy beast in his Fairmount studio for more than ten years. Garfield reaches readers in more than 2,500 newspapers from over one hundred countries. The prank-loving cat has also been the subject of more than eleven best-selling books, three television specials, the model for some five thousand Garfield items, and has starred in his own film *Garfield: The Movie*. Even with all the success, Garfield is as independent and stubborn as any real-life Hoosier. "Home," says Garfield, "is where they understand you."

MINERAL RESOURCES

Coal mining flourished along the Wabash and Ohio rivers during the late 1800s. Much of central Indiana's coal deposits have been mined since that time. Still, coal remains the state's chief mineral. About 36 million tons of coal is mined each year, mostly in the southwest part of the state.

Oil was plentiful near Geneva around the beginning of the twentieth century. According to Geneva resident Otis Buckley, "Black gold played a major role in how people made a living and small villages and towns developed." Today, oil drills mostly operate west of Evansville and northeast of Indianapolis. But one of the nation's richest oil deposits is found in Whiting, in northern Indiana. Nearby, factories in East Chicago, Hammond, and Gary turn oil into petroleum products.

Large limestone deposits lie in Lawrence County. Stonecutters prefer Indiana limestone because it is easy to dig from the ground and to carve. Stone blocks from southern Indiana quarries have been carted nationwide to build such landmarks as the Chicago Art Institute, New York's Empire State Building, and the Pentagon near Washington, D.C.

Workers from the "land of limestone" claim that stonework is in their blood. "When I was a boy, there were ordinary families and there were stone families," wrote Jack Kendall in his book *In Stone Country*. "I came from a stone family . . . every morning I'd sit down to breakfast and all the talk was stone, stone, stone."

2002 GROSS STATE PRODUCT: $205 Million

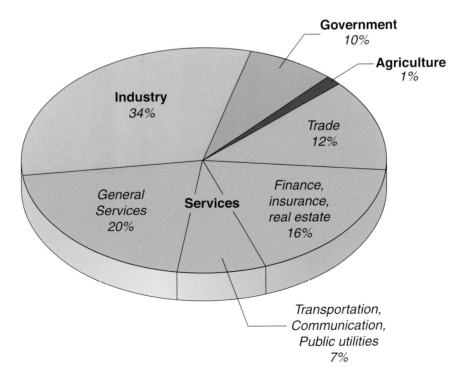

Government 10%

Agriculture 1%

Industry 34%

Trade 12%

General Services 20%

Services

Finance, insurance, real estate 16%

Transportation, Communication, Public utilities 7%

Chapter Six

Hoosier Highlights

Indiana seems like a state with a sense of humor. It's one of those strange places where a city named South Bend is in the north part of the state and North Vernon is in the south. Towns in Indiana flatlands are named after mountainous locations like Peru and Geneva. The oddest name is Santa Claus. The town's post office receives half a million letters each December addressed to the red-suited, bearded legend.

Another unusual Indiana feature is the number of places with the same name. For example, Indiana claims four Buena Vistas and four Salems. There are even two Pumpkin Centers.

State highways connect most good-sized cities. Still, finding unusual hideaways can be tricky. This is no hardship for visitors, though. From south to north, Hoosiers befriend travelers—whether they are lost or not.

Hoosierland is a blend of rough industrial cities and quiet farm communities. Outside of the Indianapolis area, most towns rarely reach bumper-to-bumper conditions. But whatever the size, Indiana cities look and feel like small towns.

The Whitewater Canal, built between 1840 and 1860, moved both passengers and freight between the Whitewater Valley and Ohio River. Today, visitors can ride a horse-drawn canal boat.

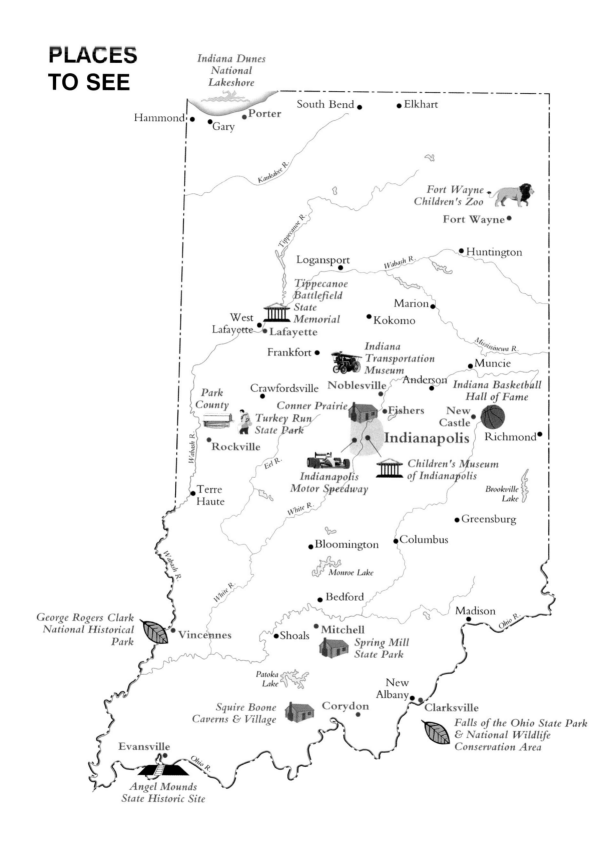

PLACES TO SEE

Indiana Dunes
National
Lakeshore

Hammond

Gary

Porter

South Bend

Elkhart

Kankakee R.

Fort Wayne
Children's Zoo

Fort Wayne

Huntington

Tippecanoe R.

Logansport

Wabash R.

Tippecanoe
Battlefield
State
Memorial

Marion

West
Lafayette

Lafayette

Kokomo

Mississinewa R.

Frankfort

Indiana
Transportation
Museum

Muncie

Anderson

Park
County

Crawfordsville

Noblesville

Indiana Basketball
Hall of Fame

Conner Prairie

Turkey Run
State Park

Fishers

New
Castle

Indianapolis

Richmond

Wabash R.

Rockville

Eel R.

Indianapolis
Motor Speedway

Children's Museum
of Indianapolis

Brookville
Lake

Terre
Haute

White R.

Greensburg

Bloomington

Columbus

Monroe Lake

White R.

Bedford

Madison

Ohio R.

George Rogers Clark
National Historical
Park

Vincennes

Shoals

Mitchell

Spring Mill
State Park

Patoka
Lake

New
Albany

Squire Boone
Caverns & Village

Corydon

Clarksville

Falls of the Ohio State Park
& National Wildlife
Conservation Area

Evansville

Ohio R.

Angel Mounds
State Historic Site

Indiana's southern countryside has inspired countless artists with its beauty. In the early 1800s budding craftspeople were drawn to New Harmony. Art colonies soon developed around the state. By the early 1900s the largest colony developed in Brown County. Artists captured the area's forested hills in autumn, the rugged beauty of the rushing streams, homey log cabins, and scores of woodland creatures on canvas. These landscape painters became known as the Hoosier Group.

Artist Theodore Clement (T. C.) Steele loved Brown County so much that he built an eleven-room home and several art studios on 211 acres in the heart of its rolling hills and forests. His studios in Belmont became one of the nation's most celebrated artists' colonies. Today, the studios are open to visitors as a state historic site. A host of landscape artists, potters, quilters, and weavers continue the Hoosier Group traditions. They sell their work in nearby Nashville.

The art colony encouraged performing arts as well, another tradition that continues. Indiana University runs a theater in Nashville. The town also hosts the Little Opry, named after the Grand Ole Opry in Nashville, Tennessee. Two thousand people crowd onto long rows of wooden benches to hear the finest country music this side of Tennessee.

Architectural Wonders

Fifteen miles from Nashville is the town of Columbus, an architectural marvel. Plopped between Brown County log cabins and flat Midwestern farmland are more than fifty buildings created by the world's finest architects. The First Christian Church was designed by top architect Eliel Saarinen in 1942. At the time, its clean lines revolutionized American church design and sparked the widespread interest in building design. Fifteen years later, the Cummins Engine Foundation in Columbus agreed to pay leading architects to plan new public buildings and preserve old treasures.

City leaders have adopted the motto that anything "worth building is worth building right." Now structures by design giants Harry Weese, Eero Saarinen (Eliel's son), Richard Meier, and I. M. Pei dot the city's skyline. Schools, fire stations, factories, even the county jail have bold shapes and lively colors. Sculptures by Henry Moore, Jean Tinguely, Constantino Nivola, and Robert Indiana—a proud Hoosier who adopted the state's name—enhance building plazas, riverfront parks, and shopping areas. Visitors from around the world herald Columbus as "America's architectural showplace" and "Athens of the prairie."

Columbus, noted for its unique architectural showpieces, is home to the colorful Ameritech building.

Columbus's respect and affection for architecture also embraces the fine arts and the variety of ethnic groups that create them. The town of about 38,000 people supports an arts center, a dance company, theater productions, and the state's oldest symphony orchestra. Columbus is set on building a community "open to every race, color, and opinion."

"This group of people really cares about the community and its development," noted the architect Richard Meier. "It uses the best talent . . . for the good of the citizens."

Rooted in the Past

Many areas of southern Indiana are deeply steeped in history. A visit to Vincennes, Indiana's first town, and the restored buildings in New Harmony is like stepping into the past. Vincennes preserves Grouseland, the home of the first Indiana Territory governor and ninth president of the United States, William Henry Harrison. Nearby is Elihu Stout's print shop, the first in the Northwest Territory, complete with copies of the earliest *Indiana Gazette*.

Since 1920 the same fifty-cent toll bridge has connected New Harmony with Illinois. The town's ivy-covered buildings look as they did in the 1800s when they were built. The nation's first golden raintrees, brought here by German pioneers, edge narrow brick streets. Their unusual leafed trunks remain as green as grass, even in winter. In the third week of June they burst into bloom. Later, they shed their petals in a shower of brilliant gold.

"We still follow many German traditions," explains Velma Fisher. "Each Christmas we hide a glass pickle ornament on the tree, as our ancestors did. The person who finds the pickle receives an extra present." Townspeople also celebrate their roots during the annual Golden Raintree Festival, Heritage Week, and Kunstfest (arts festival).

"I happen to like country and woods and land with open space. I fell in love with southern Indiana," a Massachusetts-born Hoosier recalls.

Southern Indiana has many lovely spots. Madison and Newburgh are nestled in the Ohio River valley. Both picture-perfect towns recall Indiana's steamboat days. A tour of Madison includes visits to homes once owned by riverboat captains and railroad barons. In Newburgh, houses along the water still have captain's walks, where seamen kept a lookout for their boats.

To the west is the rugged country of Abraham Lincoln and Squire Boone. The Lincoln Boyhood National Memorial is the site of the village where Abe lived as a boy, complete with a working 160-acre farm and

From the ages of seven to twenty-one, Abraham Lincoln lived on a farm in Warrick County. This preserved historic site is open to visitors seeking knowledge on Lincoln's early years.

muscum. "Abraham, very large for his age, had an axe put into his hand at once; and from that moment till well into his twenty-third year, he was almost constantly handling the most useful instrument," wrote a biographer of Lincoln's Indiana days.

Squire Boone and his brother Daniel discovered awesome below-ground cave formations and waterfalls in 1790. Squire stayed to build a gristmill powered by water from the caverns. In 1973 the mill and village he founded were restored and turned into a living museum. But the greatest fun is trekking through the secret underground passageways.

"Indiana's state park system is one of the finest in the nation," said Purdue professor Harry Targ.

Hoosiers greatly enjoy the state's seven park inns. Four of these are in the south. At these popular resorts, nature lovers can hike, swim, and bird-watch. Waterfalls, rolling hills, and caverns are scattered throughout Hoosier National Forest. Interesting discoveries are everywhere—from Bedford's limestone quarries to the charm of Brown County.

CENTRAL INDIANA

Indianapolis is unusual among the nation's large cities. It prospered even though its nearby waterways were too shallow for steamboat travel. Once people scornfully called the state capital India-No-Place. Today Indianapolis hums with government, business, sports, and cultural activities.

Ringing the Capital

The hub of Indianapolis is Mile Square. In 1820 surveyor Alexander Ralston planned the capital with a mile-square center. A wide street encircled the timbered hill. Main roads fanned out from the circle like spokes on a wheel.

Now the rise is called Monument Circle. A 284-foot Soldiers and Sailors Monument, a city landmark, stands in the circle. The limestone structure, indoor museum, and surrounding statues honor Hoosier soldiers who fought in the Mexican, Civil, and Spanish-American wars.

A project to remodel government and office buildings helped Mile Square to blossom recently. In 1996 Circle Centre and the Indianapolis Artsgarden, a retail and entertainment complex, opened. Streets were repaved, trees planted, and old-fashioned lights installed. Downtown, workers renovated old apartments and converted warehouses into lofts and studios. Cafés, department stores, and art galleries opened in the area to serve the new city dwellers.

Monument Circle is located at the city center of Indianapolis. The monument above, Soldiers' and Sailors' Monument, was not added until eighty years after the circle was completed.

Not far away is Union Station, the last midwestern Victorian-style train station. Nearby is RCA Dome, where the Colts play football. Its huge nineteen-story dome stays inflated with air from twenty 100 horsepower electric fans.

Nothing excites Hoosiers more than sports. Whether professional or amateur, college or high school, hometown teams and races inspire crazy devotion from fans, better known as "Hoosier hysteria." Indianapolis is home to the state's professional teams: the Pacers (basketball), the Colts (football), and the Indianapolis Indians (baseball), a minor league team owned by the Pittsburgh Pirates. In addition, Indianapolis has Olympic-quality centers for swimming, wrestling, and cycling to enable big-name national events. The sport-crazed town is known as the "amateur sports capital," with more sports associations and halls of fame than any other city in the nation. As one reporter wrote, "Indianapolis never met a sport it didn't like."

In Indiana, high school basketball is much like a religion. Entire towns close down for school basketball games. The high school basketball game is a time when small towns can compete with big-city Hoosiers and possibly win—or at least it was until 1996. That's when the Indiana High School Athletic Association ended the eighty-five-year-old system of having all teams play in a single league. Instead, the association sorted the state's 382 teams into four tournaments by school size.

Fans were deeply divided. Many agreed that the divisions might benefit smaller schools. With fewer talented players to choose from and less money to spend, these schools tended to lose games with large schools repeatedly. One fourteen-year-old basketball player said, "I'd rather be winning."

Older Hoosiers proudly recall Milan's 1954 win over Muncie, a school fifteen times Milan's size. Five Milan boys started their careers shooting balls into peach baskets and went on to become state champions. Milan's lucky season sparked the movie *Hoosiers*.

"Everyone says Milan was forty years ago," said Larry Bundy. Bundy played for Knightstown, a school of 404 students, over thirty-five years ago and doesn't miss a sectional game. "To me, there's a Milan every year because almost each season a small school gets to the Sweet 16 [sectional], and everyone is pulling for them." Now that's Hoosier pride!

Indianapolis's greatest fame comes from the Indianapolis 500, held in May. On the Sunday before Memorial Day, 350,000 eager fans pack the Indianapolis Motor Speedway for the world's most famous long-distance automobile race. Any time of year, however, the Speedway Museum Hall of Fame, located in the center of the track, displays trophies, helmets, photos, and racing cars. Young and old can feel the thrill of the 500 by circling the track on a tour bus or by climbing into cars that belonged to famous drivers.

The arts have mushroomed in Indianapolis as well. The new Circle Theatre houses the Indianapolis Symphony Orchestra. The Indiana Repertory Theatre stages plays in a renovated movie palace. The Indianapolis Opera Company performs to sellout crowds at the city's Murat Theatre. And the Madam Walker Urban Life Center offers African-American theater and jazz concerts in a building that once housed Walker's beauty products empire.

North of Monument Circle is the Children's Museum, the largest hands-on playground in the world. Visitors can wind through a replica limestone cave, ride an old-fashioned carousel, explore an Egyptian tomb, and travel into space. Museum developers wanted a place "where children grow up and adults don't have to."

In 1977 Indianapolis began developing White River State Park. Eleven years later, the Indianapolis Zoo opened there with two thousand animals. Today the zoo features an indoor desert setting for reptiles and dolphin shows.

At the entrance to the park are the Eiteljorg Museum and Indiana State Museum. The Eiteljorg's large collection of paintings from the American West and of Native American handiwork is exceptional for the Midwest. The Indiana State Musuem traces the cultural and natural history of the entire state.

A group of children with their teacher perform an electrical experiment at Indiana's Children's Museum.

Ten miles east of Marion County in Greenfield is the birthplace of the famous poet James Whitcomb Riley. The ten-room frame house pays tribute to the man who recorded nineteenth-century Indiana at its best. The porch view reveals the setting that must have triggered Riley's lively imagination. This was the same porch where "Little Orphant Annie" warned the children,

An' the Gobble-uns 'at gits you
    Ef you
        Don't
            Watch
                Out!

"Everybody knows that Connor Prairie is one of the best, most realistic living museums in the country," exclaims traveler Richard Benjamin.

This pioneer village recalls the days when William Conner was an Indian trader and Hamilton County's earliest white settler. Men, women, and children in knee britches and long skirts reenact life in Prairietown, the 1836 historic village. Dressed as schoolmarms, carpenters, and blacksmiths, they teach school, work with wood, and hammer heated iron to shape tools. Visitors can see how pioneers made candles and soap, played dulcimers, and wove cloth.

Covered Bridge Country

The hills and forested ravines of Putnam County open onto the flat farmland of west-central Indiana. This is Parke County, known for maple syrup, mushrooms, and, most of all, covered bridges. Thirty-three covered bridges cross the region's many zigzagging streams. That's more covered bridges than in any other county in the country!

In the early 1830s covered bridges began to make their appearance in Indiana. It is believed that there were as many as five hundred in the state. Today, ninety-one remain.

PARKE COUNTY HAUNTED BRIDGE

Legend has it that the Sim Smith covered bridge in Parke County is haunted. Once, as a young girl and her uncle approached the bridge, they heard a buggy racing toward them from the other side. The uncle stopped his horse and buggy, and they waited. The hoofbeats grew louder and faster, but no buggy appeared. Then the sounds stopped suddenly. After a few minutes the pair drove through the empty bridge—too scared to talk about what had happened.

All but ten of Parke County's bridges are still safe for travel. The longest single-lane covered bridge in the world crosses a winding stream in Turkey Run State Park. Three rebuilt bridges have been moved to Billie Creek Village in Rockville. The town is at the center of Parke County's ten-day Covered Bridge Festival. The event is held in October when the treasured bridges are framed by the brilliant colors of fall.

TEN LARGEST CITIES

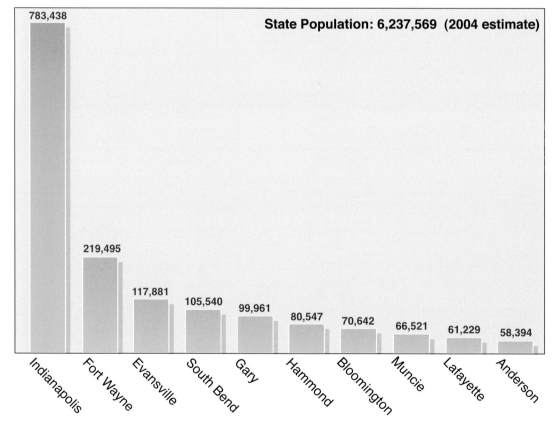

State Population: 6,237,569 (2004 estimate)

City	Population
Indianapolis	783,438
Fort Wayne	219,495
Evansville	117,881
South Bend	105,540
Gary	99,961
Hammond	80,547
Bloomington	70,642
Muncie	66,521
Lafayette	61,229
Anderson	58,394

In 1821 John Tipton surveyed the region along the shores of Lake Michigan. He noted afterward that he doubted the area "would ever be of much service to our state." Not true, said Octave Chanute. He conducted the first glider experiments from these secluded sand dunes. Chanute's 1896 flight in a heavier-than-air machine inspired Millville-born Wilbur Wright and his brother, Orville, to build their own successful glider four years later.

Dunes and Smokestacks

Today the region is packed with steel mills, marinas, shopping malls, and neighborhoods of small homes. City dwellers come from as far away as Chicago to pick blueberries, peaches, and apples in Porter County orchards. Beyond the fruit farms lies the second busiest national park east of the Rocky Mountains.

Indiana Dunes National Lakeshore is a year-round haven for sports fans and nature lovers. There are hiking and biking trails, beaches, and a nature center. Campgrounds are open in summer, and cross-country ski trails run through the snow in winter. The Paul H. Douglas Center for Environmental Education houses informative programs for children throughout the year.

Fort Wayne

Fort Wayne, Indiana's second largest city, is a major industrial center. Its population of 219,000 supports almost four hundred factories. Although business comes first in Fort Wayne, people there have always made time to relax. In 1883 Fort Wayne hosted the first lighted night baseball game played by a professional team, the Quincy Professionals. It is only fitting that Hoosier Albert von Tilzer, whose real name was Albert Gumm, or Gummblinsky, wrote the music for the popular song, "Take Me Out to the Ball Game."

Even though Fort Wayne sits in the heart of soybean country, the town has some outstanding showplaces. Historic Fort Wayne is an exact copy of

Historically known as Kekionga, the capital of the Miami Nation, Fort Wayne was named for General Anthony Wayne who captured the fort in 1794 from the Miami and named it after himself.

the original 1816 military fort. Actors dressed in period clothes go about normal nineteenth-century activities. They perform military exercises and everyday chores like baking bread, smoking meat, and shaping hot iron into horseshoes.

Fort Wayne's Lincoln Museum holds the world's largest private collection of paintings, letters, and photographs about the sixteenth president. The library contains ten thousand books in twenty-six languages about Abraham Lincoln. Many objects on display came from Lincoln's children. Lincoln's son Robert Todd gave the museum the photograph of his father that appears on the five-dollar bill. The museum bought more pictures in 1985, after the death of Robert Beckwith, Lincoln's great-grandson and the end of the Lincoln family line.

Fort Wayne's Children's Zoo may be small, but it receives worldwide applause for its landscaping and exhibit design. The Australian wildlife exhibit contains a twenty-thousand-gallon Great Barrier Reef aquarium, the largest on the North American continent. Visitors delight in observing more than five hundred animals from every part of the world in thirty-eight different habitats.

Science Central is a special Indiana museum. The aim there is to have fun with science and math. Hands-on exhibits invite children and adults to walk on the moon, drop from a parachute, or ride a high-rail bike twenty feet off the ground. The museum even hosts summertime Camp Invention and a spring science carnival. At Science Central children are encouraged to ask questions!

Clowning Around in Peru

From 1884 until 1930 seven major world circuses wintered near Peru, Indiana, an industrial community of 13,000 people. Thousands of people from miles around loved to watch the performers and animals train. In 1958 townspeople revived Peru's rich circus heritage with its Circus City Festival.

The first festival was small—a parade downtown and a few free acts on the courthouse lawn. Today almost two thousand people stage festival events for nearly 40,000 visitors. About 220 Miami County youngsters, ages seven to twenty-one, perform all the acts! They tumble and fly on trapezes, high wires, and motorcycles, while "kiddie clowns" cavort around the arena. The celebration ends with a huge parade of more than one hundred circus wagons and a fifty-piece band.

The Peru Festival began as a summer recreation program for kids. Organizers soon expanded the circus when they saw how children gained strength, confidence, and new skills. About twenty-five young Peru performers have graduated to professional circus careers.

"The bonds that form among the kids are amazing," said head trainer Bill Anderson. "Our kids get to do things most kids only dream about."

Such pride seems to be a part of most Hoosiers. People who move away carry a bit of Indiana with them. And those who move into the state tend to settle in for good. As transplanted New Yorker Irving Liebowitz wrote in *My Indiana*, "Here are proud people . . . full of noisy patriotism, perhaps, but ruggedly independent. This is where livin' is easy. I never had it so good."

THE FLAG: The Indiana state flag shows nineteen gold stars, a flaming gold torch, and the word "Indiana" in gold on a field of blue. The torch stands for liberty and enlightenment. The thirteen stars in the outer circle represent the original thirteen states. The five stars in the lower inner circle represent the next five states to be admitted to the union. The large star above the torch stands for Indiana.

THE SEAL: The state seal shows a pioneer chopping down a tree, and a bison running off in the foreground. The sun gleams over a hill in the background. The words "Seal of the State of Indiana" are displayed above the picture, and the year of Indiana statehood, 1816, is shown below. The seal was officially adopted in 1963.

State Survey

Statehood: December 11, 1816

Origin of Name: Indiana means "land of the Indians." The U.S. Congress named the state for the large number of Native Americans living there when the settlers arrived.

Nickname: The Hoosier State

Capital: Indianapolis

Motto: The Crossroads of America

Flower: Peony

Tree: Tulip tree

Bird: Cardinal

Stone: Salem limestone

Peony

Cardinal

ON THE BANKS OF THE WABASH, FAR AWAY

Composer Paul Dresser was born in Terre Haute, on the banks of the Wabash. He wrote his most famous song, "On the Banks of the Wabash," in 1899. Within a year of its composition it had sold over one million copies of sheet music—an amazing amount for this prephonograph era. In 1913 it was adopted as the official state song.

By Paul Dresser

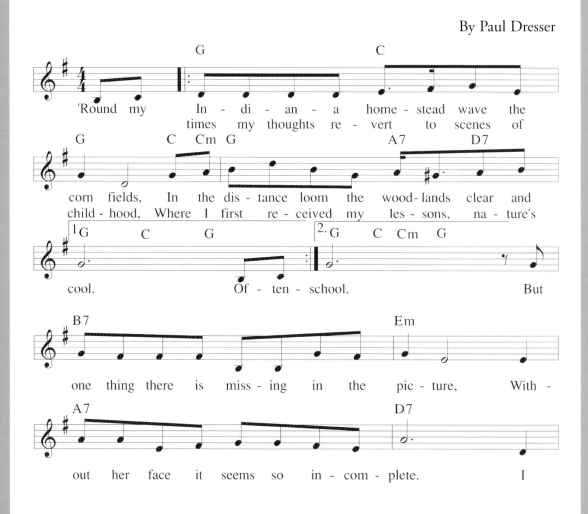

Highest Point: 1,257 feet above sea level near Bethel

Lowest Point: 320 feet above sea level along the Ohio River in Posey County

Area: 36,291 square miles

Greatest Distance North to South: 265 miles

Greatest Distance East to West: 140 miles

Bordering States: Michigan to the north, Kentucky to the south, Ohio to the east, and Illinois to the west

Hottest Recorded Temperature: 116 degrees Fahrenheit at Collegeville on July 14, 1936

Coldest Recorded Temperature: -36 degrees Fahrenheit at New Whiteland on January 19, 1994

Average Annual Precipitation: 40 inches

Major Rivers: Big Blue, Calumet, Eel, Elkhart, Iroquois, Kankakee, Maumee, Ohio, Patoka, Saint Joseph, Tippecanoe, Wabash, White, Whitewater

Major Lakes: Brookville, Freeman, Manitou, Maxinkuckee, Monroe, Patoka, Prairie Creek, Raccoon, Salamonie, Shafer, Tippecanoe, Wawasee

Trees: ash, hickory, maple, pecan, red oak, walnut, white oak, yellow poplar (tulip tree)

Wild Plants: aster, bladderwort, corn cockle, fringed gentian, golden-rod, iris, jack-in-the-pulpit, orchid, oxeye daisy, peony, pitcher plant, prickly pear cactus, pussy willow, Queen Anne's lace, round-leaved sundew, sunflower, sweet clover, violet

Animals: beaver, fox, opossum, rabbit, raccoon, skunk, squirrel, weasel, white-tailed deer

Weasel

Gray bats

Birds: bald eagle, bluebird, blue jay, cardinal, duck, great horned owl, hummingbird, mourning dove, peregrine falcon, pileated woodpecker, quail, robin, ruffed grouse, swift, wild turkey

Fish: bass, bluegill, carp, catfish, crappie, perch, salmon, sunfish, trout

Endangered Animals: bald eagle, fat pocketbook pearly mussel, gray bat, Indiana bat, interior least tern, Kirtland's warbler, orange-foot pimpleback, peregrine falcon, pink mucket, piping plover, rough pigtoe, white cat's paw pearly mussel, white wartyback

Endangered Plants: mead's milkweed, pitcher's thistle, running buffalo clover

TIMELINE

Indiana History

c. 1000 BCE Mound Builders begin to develop communities in present-day Indiana.

c. 1450 The large prehistoric structure at Angel Mounds stands empty.

1679 French explorer René-Robert Cavalier, Sieur de La Salle journeys down the Saint Joseph River to the site of modern-day South Bend.

1732 Indiana's oldest permanent community is established at Vincennes by the French.

1751 The Miami leader Little Turtle is born at the site of present-day Fort Wayne.

1755 The French and Indian War begins with the French and British fighting for control of the fur trade.

1763 All of present-day Indiana becomes part of the British Empire as the French and Indian War ends with a British victory; British forts in Indiana are captured by Native Americans during Pontiac's Rebellion.

1775–1783 The American Revolution is fought.

1778 A force of Americans under George Rogers Clark captures Vincennes from the British.

1787 Indiana becomes part of the Northwest Territory, an area that will eventually become five states.

1791 Troops under General Arthur St. Clair are ambushed by Native Americans led by Little Turtle; the Americans lose over six hundred men.

1794 General Anthony Wayne defeats a Native American force at the Battle of Fallen Timbers on the Maumee River in Ohio, moves up the Maumee River, and builds Fort Wayne.

1800 The Indiana Territory is created with its capital at Vincennes.

1809 Territorial governor William Henry Harrison receives some 3 million acres from various Native American groups in Indiana after a treaty is signed at Fort Wayne.

1811 Troops commanded by William Henry Harrison, who later became the ninth president, defeat Native Americans in the Battle of Tippecanoe.

1812–1814 The War of 1812 is fought.

1816 Indiana becomes the nineteenth state. The family of seven-year-old Abraham Lincoln moves from Kentucky to Indiana.

1822 Construction of the Wabash and Erie Canal begins at Fort Wayne.

1824 Indianapolis becomes the capital of Indiana.

1825 Followers of Robert Owen come to New Harmony and found the state's first free school, free kindergarten, and coeducational school.

1845 John "Johnny Appleseed" Chapman dies and is buried at Fort Wayne.

1861–1865 The Civil War rages between the North and the South.

1863 Confederate general John Morgan and 2,500 troops raid southern Indiana.

1888 Benjamin Harrison is elected twenty-third president of the United States.

1917 The United States enters World War I; more than 100,000 Hoosiers serve in the armed forces during the war.

1941 The United States enters World War II; about 338,000 Hoosiers serve in the war.

1949 School desegregation is ordered by Indiana's general assembly.

1965 Mitchell's Virgil "Gus" Grissom orbits the earth in the first Gemini spacecraft.

1967 Richard Hatcher is elected the state's first African-American mayor in Gary.

1970 Indianapolis Mayor Richard Lugar establishes Unigov, the program that merges Indianapolis city and surrounding governments and saves money to improve services.

1996 Julia Carson makes history as the first Indianapolis black and woman elected to the U.S. House of Representatives.

2002 Indiana State Museum, one of the largest indoor sites in the state, opens in Indianapolis at White River State Park.

2004 Mitch Daniels Jr. returns from working as President George W. Bush's director of Management and Budget to become Indiana governor.

2005 Danica Patrick becomes the only woman to race in the Indy 500, and she places fourth.

Agricultural Products: apples, cattle, chickens, corn, dairy products, eggs, hay, hogs, popcorn, oats, rye, soybeans, tobacco, tomatoes, turkeys, wheat

Manufactured Products: agricultural and industrial chemicals, aircraft parts, automobile parts, communications equipment, electrical instruments, farm machinery, iron and steel, medical supplies, musical instruments, other metals, processed foods, mobile homes, travel trailers and campers, wood cabinets

Cattle

Natural Resources: bituminous coal, clay, crushed stone, gypsum, iron slag, lime, limestone, natural gas, oil, peat, sand and gravel, timber

Business and Trade: communications, insurance, tourism, real estate, technology, transportation, wholesale and retail sales

CALENDAR OF CELEBRATIONS

James Dean Birthday Celebration Every February, actor James Dean's hometown of Marion celebrates his birthday with refreshments and a free showing of one of his films.

Maple Sugar Time This March festival in Merrillville celebrates the annual collection of sap and how it is processed into maple syrup. There are movies and tours and pure maple syrup and candy to buy.

Mountain Men Rendezvous Held in April at Bridgeton, this festival recreates a gathering of Indiana frontiersmen. Mountain men display handmade crafts and blankets and tell stories by the campfire.

Spirit of Vincennes Rendezvous At this May festival people dressed as Revolutionary War soldiers reenact battles, play fifes and drums, and prepare foods as in the 1700s.

Indiana State Pickin' and Fiddlin' Contest The state's best guitar, banjo, harmonica, and fiddle players meet at this June festival in Petersburg. Old-time singers and bluegrass bands add to the musical treats.

Clay City Pottery Festival In June the only working stoneware pottery works in Indiana at Clay City offers tours to show how pottery is made. The festival also displays crafts, antique cars, and tractors.

Woodland Nations Powwow The Miami people of Indiana host this June event in Muncie. Native American music, foods, and crafts are all a part of this weekend celebration.

Indiana Avenue Jazz Heritage Festival Held in August in Indianapolis, this festival features local and national jazz musicians. Visitors find lots of food, arts and crafts, and even a showcase for young musicians.

Watermelon Festival Brownstown celebrates its favorite summer treat in this August festival. There are crafts and entertainment, plenty of watermelon, and, of course, a seed-spitting contest.

Ligonier Marshmallow Festival This eastern Indiana town lays claim to the world's largest marshmallow. Crafts, food, parades, and rides can be found at this September festival.

Feast of the Hunters' Moon This weekend festival at Fort Ouiatenon Historic Park in Lafayette celebrates the life of Indiana's early French traders and Native Americans. During the late September/early October event crowds gather to see crafts, costumes, and games—including tomahawk-throwing contests.

Covered Bridge Festival Every October during this celebration, Rockville residents offer visitors a map to visit the area's beautiful covered bridges and fall colors. In town, guests can find arts and crafts, music, and local foods like sweet corn and funnel cakes.

International Festival Cultures from around the world gather at this festival held at Indianapolis in October. There are plenty of ethnic foods to taste as well as ethnic entertainment.

Festival of Gingerbread Everybody from children to professionals can compete in a gingerbread decorating contest at this Fort Wayne festival. Held in late November and early December, the celebration also features caroling and holiday lights.

STATE STARS

Julia Carson (1938–) became the first black and the first woman U.S. Congressperson to represent Indianapolis in 1996. Since then, she has introduced laws to fund schools, improve health care and food safety, and block kids from acquiring guns.

John "Johnny Appleseed" Chapman (1774–1845) is famous for his travels through the Ohio, Indiana, and Illinois territories, where he planted numerous apple orchards. Chapman is buried in Fort Wayne.

Joshua Bell (1967–) started playing violin at age five and made his professional debut with the Philadelphia Orchestra at age fourteen. Since then, the Bloomington musician has released thirteen albums and has played in two movies and has performed with countless symphonies and famous conductors worldwide.

Larry Bird (1956–) is one of basketball's all-time great players. Born in West Baden, Bird played pro basketball for thirteen years with the Boston Celtics and made basketball's All-Star Team twelve times.

Larry Bird

Frank Borman (1928–   ) of Gary was one of the first three astronauts to orbit the moon. Borman served as the commander of a famous Apollo mission in 1968 when the crew became the first people to see the back of the moon. He had also flown an earlier Gemini space mission.

Mordecai "Three Finger" Brown (1876–1948) was born in Nyesville. Although he had lost half a finger in a childhood accident, he went on to become a famous major league pitcher. Between 1906 and 1911 he averaged more than twenty wins a season for the Chicago Cubs. In 1949 Brown was named to the Baseball Hall of Fame.

Katie Hall (1938–   ) was the first black woman representative to the Indiana House of Representatives (1974–1976) and first African-American senator to the U. S. Congress from 1976–1982. In 1983 Hall introduced the bill to make Martin Luther King Jr.'s birthday a legal pubic holiday. Within a month the bill was passed and signed into law.

Hoagland "Hoagy" Carmichael (1899–1981) was one of America's best-loved songwriters. Born in Bloomington, Carmichael attended Indiana University. His hit songs included "Stardust," "Georgia on My Mind," and "Lazy River."

Tamika Catchings (1979–   ) Indiana Fever's top scorer was only one of four college females to earn Player of the Century in basketball four times. With the Fever, this Tennessee-born defender was the team's first player on the ALL-WNBA team and helped lead the U.S. National team to a gold medal at the 2002 World Basketball Championships.

William Merritt Chase (1849–1916), a famous American painter, was born in Nineveh. Chase founded the New York School of Art and painted landscapes and portraits of wealthy Americans.

Schuyler Colfax (1823–1885) served as U.S. vice president under Ulysses S. Grant from 1869 to 1873. Born in New York, Colfax moved to South Bend as a boy. He served in Congress as a representative from Indiana before becoming vice president.

Jim Davis (1945–   ), the creator of everybody's favorite cartoon cat, Garfield, was born in Marion. Garfield appears in some five hundred newspapers and also had his own Saturday morning television show.

James Dean (1931–1955) of Marion had a promising movie-acting career that was cut short by a tragic car accident. Dean starred in *East of Eden, Rebel without a Cause,* and *Giant.*

Eugene Debs (1855–1926) of Terre Haute was a powerful American labor leader. Debs formed the American Railway Union and supported one of the first large-scale strikes in the United States, the Pullman strike. In 1894 railway workers across the United States went on strike in support of workers at the Pullman Company in Chicago, which built railroad cars. Debs also ran as a socialist for U.S. president five times.

Bob Griese (1945–   ) is one of football's best-known quarterbacks. Born in Evansville, Griese played college football at Purdue then led the Miami Dolphins to Super Bowl victories in 1973 and 1974.

Benjamin Harrison (1833–1901) was the twenty-third president of the United States. Born in Ohio, Harrison moved to Indianapolis as a young man and is buried there in Crown Hill Cemetery. He was the grandson of the ninth president, William Henry Harrison.

William Henry Harrison (1773–1841) served as governor of the Indiana Territory and then as the ninth president of the United States. Harrison died from pneumonia after only a month in office.

Richard Hatcher (1933–   ) of Michigan City was one of the first African-American mayors of a large American city. Hatcher served as mayor of Gary from 1967 to 1987.

Jimmy Hoffa (1913–1975?) was born in the town of Brazil. A famous labor leader, Hoffa served as president of the Teamsters Union from 1958 to 1971. Hoffa mysteriously disappeared in 1975 and is believed to have been murdered.

Michael Jackson (1958–   ) and his singing brothers and sisters were born in Gary. Michael was only ten years old when he had a hit record as the lead singer for the Jackson Five. As a solo artist, Jackson gained international superstar status, and his album *Thriller* became the best-selling album of all time.

Janet Jackson (1966–   ), youngest of nine from the same Gary musical family as Michael, is a pop and rhythm and blues star with several top hits selling more than 40 million albums. Janet has three Grammy awards and an Oscar nomination. She has acted on several television shows and was the highest paid recording star of all time in 1997.

Janet Jackson

David Letterman (1947–), late night TV's wacky talk-show host, was born in Indianapolis. Letterman went to Ball State University and began his showbiz career as a radio and television announcer in his hometown. He has won a number of Emmies for his popular talk show.

Little Turtle (1751–1812) was a well-regarded leader of the Miami people of Indiana. Little Turtle led several victorious attacks against U.S. troops before he was defeated in the Battle of Fallen Timbers in 1794. After that he supported peace. He was born near the Eel River.

Shelley Long (1949–) is a well-liked comic actress from Fort Wayne who starred in the popular 1980s television show *Cheers* and the 1995 movie *The Brady Bunch*.

John Cougar Mellencamp (1951–), singer and songwriter, was born in Seymore. His pop songs often tell of small-town life. Mellencamp's hits include "Jack and Diane" and "Scarecrow."

Robert Owen (1801–1877) was an Indiana politician and social reformer. As a member of the U.S. Congress, Owen helped found the Smithsonian Institution. He also helped establish Indiana's free school system. Owen's letter to President Lincoln in 1862 played a part in Lincoln's decision to emancipate America's slaves.

Cole Porter (1891–1964) was a songwriter whose hits included "Night and Day" and "I've Got You under My Skin." He also wrote many musicals, including *Kiss Me, Kate*. He was born in Peru.

Gene Stratton Porter (1868–1924) was a writer of nature books and fictional works. Her novels *Freckles* and *The Girl of the Limberlost* were about life in the Limberlost marsh area of northern Indiana where she lived.

J. Danforth Quayle (1947–   ) served as vice president of the United States from 1989 to 1993 under President George H. W. Bush. Born in Indianapolis, Quayle was a U.S. representative and senator from Indiana before becoming vice president.

James Whitcomb Riley (1849–1916), the "Hoosier Poet," was born in Greenfield. Riley's poetry was written in simple language and appealed to a large number of readers. His works included "The Old Swimmin' Hole," "Little Orphant Annie," and "The Raggedy Man."

Oscar Robertson (1938–   ) is a basketball standout from Indianapolis. At Crispus Attucks High School, Robertson helped his team become the first in Indiana history to have an unbeaten season. He was on the gold-medal-winning U.S. Olympic team in 1960, then went on to play pro ball for the Cincinnati Royals and the Milwaukee Bucks.

Knute Rockne (1888–1931) gained fame as a football coach for his exciting style of play and his winning record. As the coach at Notre Dame from 1918 to 1931, Rockne lost only 12 games while winning 105. The legendary coach was born in Norway.

Red Skelton (1913–1997) won fame as a comedian playing a number of zany characters such as Clem Kadiddlehopper and Freddie the Freeloader. Skelton entertained on radio and television and in the movies. He was born in Vincennes.

Clement (1831–1901) and **John** (1833–1917) **Studebaker** were brothers who began making horse-drawn carriages in South Bend in the mid-1800s. Their company started producing electric vehicles in 1902 and gasoline automobiles in 1904.

Tecumseh (1768–1813), a great Shawnee leader, hoped to drive white settlers from the Indiana region. He gathered a force of Native Americans at a village on the Tippecanoe River, only to have his force defeated by an American army while Tecumseh, himself, was away.

Twyla Tharp (1941–) earned fame as a dancer and choreographer. She was born in Portland but is known nationwide for her dance company and dance numbers developed for theater, television, and ice shows.

Kurt Vonnegut Jr. (1922–) uses fantasy to tell of the darker side of human life in his novels. His works include *Slaughterhouse Five* and *Breakfast of Champions.* Vonnegut was born in Indianapolis.

Sarah Breedlove Walker (1867–1919) moved to Indianapolis in 1910. Known as Madam C. J. Walker, she founded a company that made hair-care products for African-American women and that created many good jobs for them. Walker became the first black woman millionaire, supporting many charities.

Ryan White (1971–1990) was the first person with enough courage to talk about AIDS in public. The Kokomo eighth grader bravely battled neighbors who wrongly feared catching the disease from him. He addressed Congress, met with celebrities, and spoke out on television and in headline interviews, putting a face on this terrible disease.

Ryan White

Fort Wayne's Children's Zoo (Fort Wayne) Exhibits at this zoo include the Indonesian Rain Forest, Orangutan Valley, and the Australian Adventure. The zoo also has the world's only Endangered Species Carousel.

Lincoln Museum (Fort Wayne) Exhibits depict Lincoln's life from his childhood in Indiana to his presidency. Using computers, visitors can read Lincoln's mail, fight in a Civil War battle, or take a history quiz.

Historic Fort Wayne (Fort Wayne) The log buildings here look as they would have in 1816. Visitors can learn about the life of soldiers at the old fort and view artifacts that belonged to General Anthony Wayne and the Miami chief Little Turtle.

Circus City Festival Museum (Peru) The history of the circus is celebrated at this museum. Posters, costumes, and other circus-related items are on display.

Levi Coffin House State Historic Site (Fountain City) The home of Levi and Catherine Coffin was known as the "Grand Central Station of the underground railroad." More than two thousand enslaved people escaping from the South passed through the Coffin home.

Indiana Basketball Hall of Fame (New Castle) The history of Indiana basketball is featured at this museum. Displays honor state championship teams and superstars like Larry Bird.

Conner Prairie (Fishers) Life in an early 1800s Indiana village is the focus of this living-history museum. Costumed employees demonstrate everyday activities in the village's schoolhouse, general store, blacksmith shop, and other period buildings.

The Falls of the Ohio State Park and National Wildlife Conservation Area (Clarksville) Visitors to this park can view a fossil bed containing corals and other examples of prehistoric ocean life that are at least 400 million years old. There is a film on the history of the falls in the visitor center and a wildlife observation center.

The Children's Museum of Indianapolis (Indianapolis) This exciting museum offers everything from life-size Tyrannosaurus rex to a replica limestone cave to an 1800s carousel. Space travel, world history, and nature are just a few of the subjects explored at this museum.

Indianapolis Motor Speedway (Indianapolis) Visitors to the world's most famous race track can see a film on the history of the Indianapolis 500, take a bus tour of the track, and explore the displays at the speedway's museum, which include Indy cars, objects belonging to famous drivers, and antique automobiles.

Eiteljorg Museum of American Indian and Western Art (Indianapolis) Cowboys and Indians and the American West are featured at this Indianapolis museum. Sculptures and paintings from famous Western artists and artwork from Native American cultures—such as clothing, baskets, and pottery—can be viewed here.

Eiteljorg Museum

Spring Mill State Park (Mitchell) A water-powered gristmill, sawmill, post office, and boot shop are among the buildings of this reconstructed 1815 village. There is also a memorial to astronaut Virgil I. Grissom, an Indiana native, which includes a space capsule and a presentation on space exploration.

Squire Boone Caverns and Village (Corydon) The sparkling underground rock formations and waterways at this site were first discovered by Daniel Boone and his brother Squire in 1790. Pioneer crafts are demonstrated in the village's log cabins.

Lincoln Boyhood National Memorial (Lincoln City) The farm where Lincoln lived between 1816 and 1830 is preserved at this site. Visitors can tour the reconstructed homestead, the visitor center, and the grave of Lincoln's mother.

Angel Mounds State Historic Site (Evansville) Once the location of a village of prehistoric Mound Builders, the site today displays reconstructed dwellings and other buildings from 1200 CE to 1400.

Wolf Park (Battle Ground) Visitors to this unique park can see wolves and bison interact much as they would in the wild. The wolves "hunt" the bison, although they are not allowed to harm them.

Tippecanoe Battlefield State Memorial (Battle Ground) The site of William Henry Harrison's victory over Native Americans under the leadership of Tecumseh's brother, the Prophet, today has a museum to explain the events surrounding the battle. The park also offers walking trails.

Indiana Dunes National Lakeshore (Porter) The ever-shifting dunes along Lake Michigan provide a number of ways to have fun. You can hike and swim, as well as explore a nineteenth-century farm and see nature exhibits on the area's plants and wildlife.

Indiana Dunes National Lakeshore

Find Out More

If you'd like to find out more about Indiana, look in your school library, local library, bookstore, or video store. Here are some titles:

STATE BOOKS

Heinrichs, Ann. *Indiana* (America the Beautiful). Danbury, CT: Children's Press, 2000.

Ling, Bettina. *Indiana* (From Sea to Shining Sea). Danbury, CT: Children's Press, 2003.

PEOPLE AND SPECIAL-INTEREST BOOKS

Beyer, Mark. *Larry Bird* (Basketball Hall of Famers). New York: Rosen Publishing Group, 2001.

Price, Nelson. *Legendary Hoosiers.* Guild Press, 2001.

Indiana Historical Society

http://www.indianahistory.org

This guide offers historical information on the state of Indiana.

Indiana

http://www.50states.com/indiana.htm

Try this site for some fast facts on Indiana.

Division of Fish and Wildlife

http://www.in.gov/dnr/fishwild/

This site provides information regarding fishing, hunting, and endangered wildlife in Indiana. Maps and photos are also featured.

Indiana State Museum

http://www.in.gov/ism/

This site gives up-to-date information on the history of the state of Indiana through its cultural and scientific exhibits.

Index

Page numbers in **boldface** are illustrations and charts.

Marlene Targ Brill is author of more that sixty books, including *Illinois*, *Michigan*, and *Minnesota* by Marshall Cavendish. To write *Indiana*, Brill explored the far corners of the state. She interviewed city and factory workers and teachers; hiked around buffalo farms, Indian mounds, and dunes; and visited many historic sites. Then she drove home to Illinois, where she writes and lives with her husband, Richard; daughter, Alison; and puppy Kipling, also an author of sorts.